Remember Jekyll Island

Copyright © 2010 by Babs McDonald, PhD.

L*ANGDON*
S*TREET* P*RESS*

Langdon Street Press
212 3rd Avenue North, Suite 290
Minneapolis, MN 55401
612.455.2293
www.langdonstreetpress.com

ISBN - 978-1-936183-10-4
ISBN - 1-936183-10-2
LCCN - 2010926447

Cover Design and Typeset by Melanie Shellito

Printed in the United States of America

Babs McDonald

Remember Jekyll Island

Babs McDonald, PhD

Langdon Street Press
Minneapolis, MN

Remember Jekyll Island is dedicated to the thousands of citizens who have consistently and persistently opposed the recently planned commercial, timeshare, and condominium development of Jekyll Island State Park, and to those who work for the establishment, protection, and preservation of public lands everywhere.

.

Table of Contents

Acknowledgments

Many individuals helped to create *Remember Jekyll Island*. These contributors provided information, pointed me in the right direction, critiqued my writing, and offered encouragement. David and Mindy Egan improved the accuracy of the text (although all errors are mine). Dory Ingram gave me encouragement and made me laugh along the way, and reviewed drafts as the work progressed. Dr. Steve Newell provided much of the material for Chapter 4 about Jekyll Island's environment, and reviewed the chapter text. Dr. Ken Cordell contributed Chapter 10, an analysis of the science and analytical methods used by the Jekyll Island Authority to support their actions. Cliff Hickman, Michelle Cram, Jessica Nickelsen, Ian Cartwright, Susan Murphy, Barbara Keely, and Ken Forbus provided review and comments that improved the text. Greta Langhenry, completely new to the Jekyll Island issue, provided an insightful review and editing of the draft, asking for clarification where it was needed. Her edits undoubtedly made this text more complete and easier to understand. The advantage of many perspectives has made this story much more readable. I am grateful to Charles Seabrook and Janisse Ray for their critiques on the back cover. I would like to thank Madeline Van Dyke for her identification of "what is at stake" for Georgia citizens (and all citizens), outlined in Chapter 1. My thanks, as well, go to Sam Rawls, for his permission to reproduce his cartoons about Jekyll Island. Finally, I am grateful to the University of Alabama Press for providing permission to reproduce sections of the book *Southern Journeys: Tourism, history, and culture in the modern South.*

Each chapter begins with a quote from one or two of the thousands of citizens who took time to share their comments on the Initiative to Protect Jekyll Island Web site. My thanks go to every one of them, for taking the time to share their perspective.

Author's Note

January 1, 2010

On December 8, 2009, the Jekyll Island Authority announced that it had suspended its contract with Linger Longer Communities. This announcement was enthusiastically welcomed by citizens across Georgia. On that date, *Remember Jekyll Island* was almost completed and, after a few additional edits, would have been on its way to the publisher. As you read, therefore, keep in mind that this is an account of Jekyll Island's history over the past few years — a history of inappropriate planning that ultimately resulted in a failed contract. When most of these words were written, the Jekyll Island Authority was working toward a public-private partnership with Linger Longer Communities, a development company. This story shows how citizen-activism can prevail, and why it must continue regarding Jekyll Island State Park. This story will provide insight into the recent past, and by all accounts following December 8, 2009, the current and possible future *modus operandi* of the Jekyll Island Authority. Jekyll Island State Park is not yet safe from extensive development. Now, however, the events of the recent past can be a lesson for the future.

Preface

I love public land. Almost incredibly, the idea of public land was foreign to me until my college years. I had been to local parks during high school, but state and national lands were almost unknown to me. I never thought about who owned those lands and how they were managed. In a required class on outdoor recreation, I was introduced to national and state park and forest lands. I was inspired by the idea of large areas of mostly undeveloped land held in public trust for common benefit. That was thirty-three years ago. Since then, I have worked in local and federal land management agencies, and my appreciation for public land continues to grow. My concern for public land is also growing. Unfortunately, a continually expanding human population has increased pressure on all types of land, and public land is not immune to this pressure.

In my opinion, Jekyll Island State Park, Georgia, is one of the public lands under threat. This threat stems from a host of pressures, including expected ones such as ecosystem degradation and the spread of invasive plant and animal species. There is another, unexpected threat to this citizen-owned barrier island — the encroachment of unwanted and in my opinion, unneeded and inappropriate private development, under the guise of "revitalization." I call it an unexpected threat because we usually think that public lands will forever remain public. This, unfortunately, is not always true.

I was prompted to write *Remember Jekyll Island* to document the story of how these changes were planned for Jekyll Island State Park, and as a case study for other public lands under threat from private sector development and over-development. I wanted to share what I have learned, and as well share the foundation that grounds my view with fellow citizens who, like me, co-own Jekyll Island and all public lands. I wanted to raise awareness of what is at stake when our public lands are threatened or lost forever. As you read *Remember Jekyll Island*, I hope your appreciation for public lands will grow. I hope you will be moved to help protect them everywhere.

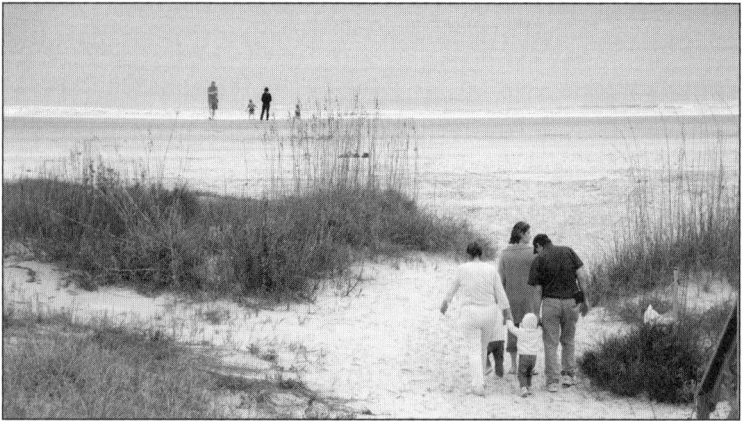

Jekyll Island has introduced generations of families to the Atlantic coast environment.

Public land is more than a physical place held in public trust. It is the concrete (if you will) embodiment of a democratic society's ideal of promoting and sustaining the health, welfare, and future of all its citizens. In a companion book to the epic documentary *National Parks: America's Best Idea*, Dayton Duncan observed of the public lands that are our national parks, "But they are more than a collection of rocks and trees and inspirational scenes from nature. They embody something less tangible yet equally enduring — an *idea*, born in the United States nearly a century after its creation, as uniquely American as the Declaration of Independence and just as radical" (2009, following the preface; emphasis in original). This statement is true for all of our public lands, including our state parks that are found in unique natural areas of every state.

Remember Jekyll Island is not affiliated with any organization or group. It is my best independent effort to tell the story of how Jekyll Island State Park is being managed in the early years of the twenty-first century. All mistakes and inaccuracies are mine. I have tried to faithfully record the story from newspaper accounts, from Georgia Open Records Act requests, from internet research, and from documented conversations with individuals involved in Jekyll Island's recent history. All photographs were taken by me. I wrote *Remember Jekyll Island* as a concerned citizen and a visitor to the state park; I do not own a home on Jekyll Island. I created *Remember Jekyll Island* in my personal capacity. The views expressed are my own and do not necessarily represent the views of the Forest Service (my employer), that of the United States Department of Agriculture, or the United States Government.

All proceeds from the sale of this book will be donated to the effort to protect Jekyll Island State Park.

Chapter 1
Why Should You Care About Jekyll Island?

K.G., Sylvania, GA — I have been vacationing on Jekyll Island since I was two years old. I love the island the way it is. It is not crowded and does not have large highways with lots of traffic. It is a place to vacation peacefully and escape the hustle and bustle of daily life. I love riding the bike trails and visiting the current shopping center. I feel safe walking on the beach or sidewalks alone or even at night. My husband, father, and brother love the golf course the way it is. We are not a wealthy family, but we can afford to vacation at Jekyll. Please do not change Jekyll Island! When I think of being there I think of such happy times and of a great little island. Please let me know if there is anything I can do to help the island stay un-commercialized and remain state-owned and controlled.

In *Remember Jekyll Island,* I outline the recent history of Jekyll Island State Park, the island known as Georgia's Jewel. The storyline, unfortunately, is familiar — a series of actions that would result in corporate financial gain from commercial development in spite of widespread citizen opposition. This time, however, the private development in question is located on land owned by the citizens of Georgia. The plan to extensively develop Georgia's barrier island state park in the face of considerable public opposition appears to challenge three American assumptions: affordable present and future access to publicly-owned land; the opportunity to authentically participate in government; and the assumption that government will act in the public trust, that is, that it will manage common resources for the public good.[1]

Access to Public Land

As a society, we often do not realize the importance of public lands to our quality of life. We take public lands for granted. We believe our public officials will ensure that public lands are always affordable and available for the highest and best use of the citizens for whom the land is held in trust. This is not always an easy task, because different people have different values and interests. Gifford Pinchot, the first Chief of the U.S. Forest Service, offered the following guidance to help resolve such conflict: "Where conflicting interests must be reconciled, the question will always be decided from the standpoint of the greatest good [for] the greatest number in the long run" (USDA Forest Service 2007).

What is the greatest good for the greatest number in the long run regarding Jekyll Island State Park? Clearly, the people of Georgia might represent the greatest number.

---

1 These concepts were contributed by Madeline Van Dyke.

Through the 10,000 plus members of a grassroots organization called the Initiative to Protect Jekyll Island (IPJI), Georgia citizens have spoken by the thousands in favor of preserving Jekyll's unique character and wildlife habitats. There are, by far, vastly more "average Georgians" in the state than there are those who can afford half-million dollar condominiums and two-hundred dollar per night hotel rooms. What is the greatest good for these citizens? The comments given in italics at the beginning of each chapter of *Remember Jekyll Island* represent what thousands of citizens believe is the greatest good for Georgians regarding Jekyll Island State Park.

The development of Jekyll Island that is being planned and executed by the Jekyll Island State Park Authority board (the governor-appointed body that sets policy for the island) does not appear to meet Pinchot's criteria for the greatest good. When private condominiums and timeshares are built beside the public beach, that beach will no longer be as easily accessible to average citizens. The land will, in effect, be privatized, accessible only to those who can afford the timeshares and condominiums occupying it. Once these residences are sold, the public land on which they were built will likely never be reclaimed for the use of average income citizens. And once a piece of land is developed, it is rarely converted back to its natural state.

On April 1, 2009, the Dublin, Georgia *Courier Herald* printed a news story with ominous news for Georgia's public lands. The paper reported:

While the Friends of Little Ocmulgee State Park prepare to hold their monthly meeting Monday at 6:30 p.m., the group's concern has shifted once again to the potential privatization of the park. According to a mass email sent out by "Friends" and obtained by the *Wheeler County Eagle*, the group is fearful that privatization legislation may be hidden within the budget currently moving through the Georgia House and Senate. (Knapp 2009)

In a follow-up story by the same publication on April 2, 2009, Holcombe noted:

State officials continue to banter about the fact that the parks aren't profitable ventures, but there's a flaw in their math and their argument. First, the parks were never intended to be cash cows. Second, by privatizing the parks we place our history and heritage at the mercy of the highest bidder.

Our state parks represent what remains of the American spirit of adventure right here in the heart of Georgia. From Warm Springs to High Falls, Cloudland Canyon to George L. Smith, these parks are a bastion for travelers and a refuge for wildlife.

If the legislature goes forth with the eventual privatization of parks like Little Ocmulgee, the only April Fools will be sitting squarely in Atlanta while the rest of us wait for the punchline.

What is at stake on Jekyll Island State Park, therefore, is greater than the reduction of public beach access and an affordable ocean vacation for average income Georgians, although this is reason enough for concern. What happens on Jekyll may foreshadow what could happen to Georgia's other state parks and those around the country. What is at stake is the continued existence of accessible state public lands, lands that are and should be the birthright of every state citizen. As Ken Burns learned during the production of his highly acclaimed documentary on national parks, and his sentiment is true for state parks as well, "Most people think the parks have always been there, that there has always been an agency charged with their care, and that — and nothing could be further from the truth — they will always be there" (2009, xv).

Public Participation in Government

In 1776, our nation's founders created a bold vision of a government established by the people, of the people, and for the people. At the heart of our government is public participation, whether it is at the ballot box, on a telephone or computer keyboard, or in the streets. We have the right to petition our government, to disagree with our government, and to expect transparency in our government.

Unfortunately, the current planning for Jekyll Island State Park's development hardly models the kind of government our nation's founders envisioned. Through the Initiative to

Protect Jekyll Island, thousands of Georgians have spoken, but it does not appear that they have been heard. Thousands have communicated through email and by phone to their elected representatives. Hundreds of citizens have traveled across Georgia to Jekyll Island to speak at the few public input sessions held; many have traveled to the State Capitol to speak directly with lawmakers. While these voices of protest have succeeded in scaling back the size of the development, the Jekyll Island Authority appears to have minimized opportunities for citizen input and influence. To be heard, citizens have fought an uphill battle, one still being fought in early 2010, and likely to continue.

The opportunity for citizens to authentically participate in their state government is at stake. The Jekyll Island Authority has moved forward with impunity. They have been encouraged to bring more development to the people's park in spite of citizen opposition. They have acted without following the best professional practices in outdoor recreation planning, a standard that citizens have a right to expect from their state government. These practices require, among other things, authentic public involvement in the planning and management of public land.

If the currently planned, and citizen opposed, Jekyll Island development is successful, what have our state officials learned about how they may conduct the public's business? Is this the message we want them to have? Authentic public participation in state government is truly at stake.

Public Trust

In an unpublished opinion editorial for the *Atlanta Journal Constitution*, State Senator Jeff Chapman wrote:

> The Georgia Code (O.C.G.A. 45-10-3(8)) states that [Jekyll Island] [A]uthority appointees should "never engage in conduct which constitutes a breach of public trust." By depriving the people's park of millions of dollars of needed revenue while enriching a private partner, and by jamming through a critically important contract without public review, the [A]uthority's leaders have violated the public's trust and compromised their standing as park stewards. Jekyll Island State Park and the people of Georgia deserve better. (Chapman 2008a)

Here is a partial list of the ways the Jekyll Island Authority has appeared, from available documentation, to challenge the public's trust. The corresponding chapter or appendix where more detail can be found is given in parentheses.

1. The Jekyll Island Authority has not appeared to follow best practices as outlined by professional standards in outdoor recreation and state park planning. (Chapters 3, 6–10)

2. The Jekyll Island Authority has moved forward with development of a fragile barrier island ecosystem without using a conservation plan to guide its development. (Chapter 4)

3. The Jekyll Island Authority has moved forward with plans for the development of a fragile barrier island ecosystem without conducting environmental assessments. (Chapter 4)

4. The Jekyll Island Authority has not appeared to have integrated publicly-funded studies and plans, such as the Georgia Statewide Comprehensive Outdoor Recreation Plan, that are relevant to the management of Georgia's public recreation lands. (Chapters 4, 6–10)

5. The Governor-appointed Jekyll Island Authority board has no members who are professionally trained in state park or outdoor recreation management. (Chapter 5)

6. The Jekyll Island Authority demolished the island's only public swimming pool; a pool which had been rebuilt with $100,000 in public funds. (Chapter 5)

7. The Jekyll Island Authority seems to have followed an unusual Request for Proposal process for selecting a private partner. (Chapter 6)

8. The Jekyll Island Legislative Oversight Committee appears to have taken on a cheerleader role for, rather than an oversight role over, the Jekyll Island Authority. (Chapter 6)

9. The Jekyll Island Authority has signed at least

two non-competitive contracts with the same consulting firm to provide analyses to inform outdoor recreation planning on public land. This firm admitted at a public forum on Jekyll Island in November 2008 that it had no staff expertise in outdoor recreation. (Chapters 6–8)

10. It does not appear that the Jekyll Island Authority has followed accepted professional planning standards in soliciting authentic public input or involvement in its proceedings, deliberations, or decisions. (Chapters 6–10)

11. The Jekyll Island Authority does not appear to be planning or managing Jekyll Island in the interest of the state's average citizens, as called for in Georgia State law. (Chapters 6–10)

12. The Jekyll Island Authority provided two contradictory explanations for how it considered a state law (PL 12-3-235) requiring a feasibility study prior to large-scale development. (Chapter 7)

13. The Jekyll Island Authority board is not representative of the people of Georgia by race or gender. (Chapter 7 and Appendix 5)

14. The Jekyll Island Authority has repeatedly contracted with, and seems to have accepted the results of, a single consulting firm's analyses, even when experts in environmental and public

land economics and outdoor recreation planning have pointed out theoretical, conceptual, and methodological shortcomings. (Chapters 8, 10)

15. By planning to build privately-owned timeshares and condominiums on public land, the Jekyll Island Authority will be, in effect, privatizing portions of public land. This is in opposition to current trends in public outdoor recreation practice. (Chapters 8, 10)

16. The (now suspended) Jekyll Island Authority — private partner contract gave favorable treatment to one developer when compared with other Jekyll Island developers. (Chapter 8)

17. The Jekyll Island Authority signed a contract that would have given ninety-nine percent of gross sales of private condominiums and timeshares to the private sector partner, while keeping only one percent for park maintenance and management. (Chapter 8)

18. The Georgia General Assembly voted to commit $50 million in taxpayer-backed bonds to support private development on Jekyll Island in the same year the state's budget was in crisis and all public teachers statewide were mandated to take a three-day furlough to save money. (Chapter 8)

The Jekyll Island Authority's apparent challenge of the

public's trust was mentioned many times by attorney and former radio talk show host Wilson Smith. On his April 1, 2008 show, Smith summed up the public trust issue:

> Another breach of the public trust by the Jekyll Island Authority is its apparent total lack of concern, bordering on scorn, for public opinion and input. It dreamed up this project, it issued a request for developers to submit proposals, and it gave its approval to Linger Longer without ever undertaking to find out first what the residents of Jekyll or what the people of the state of Georgia wanted....The Jekyll Island Authority has made a mockery of the idea that it acts as a Trustee for the people of this State.

Chapter 2
This Land is Your Land

L.H., Brunswick, GA — Jekyll Island is first and foremost a state park, and I feel that the development plans will eventually turn it into a giant amusement park (complete with plenty of pavement) for the very wealthy. The great charm of beaches, marshland, and forests will be lost forever. Is there nothing that can be done to stop the Jekyll Island Authority? I have to believe its members are profiting from this partnership in some way that may not be legal. Why else would they allow this travesty?

D.S., Athens, GA — The reason I go to Jekyll Island and love the island is because it is not developed and full of shops, stores, and condos and high rise hotels. I go to Jekyll Island to enjoy the beach and the island and the beauty and calm. If I wanted all the other distractions, I could visit any of the many cookie cutter resorts across the coastal south. I have lived in Georgia all of my life and loved Jekyll Island for its simplicity and beauty, and because there are no high-rise hotels and condos. Let the developers go somewhere else and destroy the environment and natural beauty of the coast. Leave Jekyll alone.

Public land is held in the public trust and managed by a government on behalf of and for the benefit of its citizens. When public land is mentioned, we most often think of the vast federal system of public lands and more specifically, of our national parks. All levels of government, however, hold and manage public lands. Collectively, local governments also manage an enormous area of public land in the form of local community parks, vest pocket parks, and regional parks.

Remember Jekyll Island is about public land that is managed by state government. State governments manage various types of public land. The best known and loved of these are our state parks. Generally, state parks have been modeled after national parks, and the state park movement followed the establishment of the first national parks in the early and middle years of the twentieth century. (Georgia's Indian Springs Park, surprisingly, is considered the nation's first state park. It preceded the establishment of our first national park, and was purchased as state recreation land in 1825. It did not, however, receive the official title of state park until 1931 (Georgia Department of Natural Resources, 2009a)).

Typically, state parks are a combination of natural, mostly undeveloped or lightly-developed land with affordable outdoor recreation amenities. They often are located in areas of special statewide natural, historical, or cultural interest, similar to their big sister national parks. State parks, like all public lands, are set aside for their unique features, and therefore are special places.

Jekyll Island is valued for its Loggerhead turtle nesting habitat, which requires a darkened beach during nesting season.

Regardless of whether public land is federal, state, or local, Americans hold public land dear. James Hansen, in a foreword to a small collection of essays on public land, noted that, "Public lands are part of a priceless American heritage. America is distinctive in her commitment to preserving her land for generations of Americans and millions of world visitors" (Hansen 2002, Foreword, n.p.). In the same volume, Steven G. Maurer observed that:

No other nation can claim that almost one-third of its lands belongs to its citizens. No other country has so many national forests, national wildlife refuges, national parks and monuments, national conservation areas, state parks, wilderness areas, wild and scenic

rivers — a treasure chest of public lands unmatched by
any nation on Earth. Lands that belong to the rich and
the poor, to ranchers and city dwellers, to miners and
environmentalists, to lumbermen and congressmen
— to all of us. (Maurer 2002, Introduction, n.p.)

The idea of public lands is closely connected to the
American ideals of freedom, community, and democracy.
Maurer revealed the special symbolism and multiple values
of American public land when he reflected:

> We Americans have a unique, priceless gift to pass
> on to future generations. That gift is our public land
> legacy, which lies not only in the lands themselves,
> but also in the freedom those lands symbolize....
> Like all of our freedoms, the freedom represented
> by public lands is not a given. There are those who
> think we have too much public land, who would sell
> portions of it to the highest bidder, who would give
> parts of it away... (Maurer 2002, Introduction, n.p.)

Jekyll Island State Park is so loved by her visitors that
over ten thousand of them have protested against her further
development by the private sector, their cries seeming to
fall on the deaf ears of public officials who should be
managing the park in the public trust. In *Remember Jekyll
Island*, we explore the unfortunate precedent that may be
set, diminishing opportunities for all people who value
access to their public land.

Jekyll Island State Park is not alone in the threat that it faces. A disturbing trend has emerged over the past decade, according to the national non-profit organization, Defense of Place. Established in 1997, Defense of Place works to reverse the trend in which "more and more land designated as parks, nature preserves, wilderness, and wildlife refuges is being sold and developed....In an effort to balance shrinking budgets or to make way for 'progress,' elected officials and private institutions are selling off land dedicated to remain forever wild. When they do, they break a pact with future generations" (In Defense of Place 2008).

There are, of course, a multitude of threats to public lands, including state parks. Environmental threats such as

According to Georgia state law, Jekyll Island State Park should remain affordable and accessible to future generations of Georgia citizens.

soil erosion, air pollution, invasive species, habitat destruction, and climate change degrade the natural beauty and integrity of our public lands. In spite of these grave threats, however, often the greatest danger faced by public lands comes from development. In most cases, the offending development is outside of the public land boundary. Since land does not recognize the legal boundaries we humans place on it, private development's impacts may be felt for miles around, including within nearby public lands. When public lands are turned over to the private sector without appropriate oversight or control, however, the threat of development comes from within, like a cancer.

Parts of Jekyll Island State Park, unfortunately, may be in danger of succumbing to the cancer of public land privatization in the twenty-first century. The park's story is the story of similar threats to public lands nationwide. In the chapters that follow, I will introduce you to Jekyll Island State Park, her history, and the current fight for her future. As the only accessible barrier island in Georgia owned by the public, her citizen benefits cover the range of those attributed to the most treasured of public lands, our national parks. Also like our national parks, Jekyll Island provides environmental and ecological benefits to her citizens and to the plants and animals that call the island home. Precisely because of these amenities and benefits, Jekyll Island has been in the crosshairs of public servants and partner-developers who would degrade her state park character with private condominiums, timeshares, hotels, and an expanded and upscale retail center, resulting in significant private sector financial gain, and a resulting loss to the public.

Citizen Action and Public Land

Today is a Sunday. As I write this, the United States Senate is convening. It is convening on this weekend day to discuss and vote on the addition of land to the National Wilderness Preservation System, which is one of the most unique of our federal public land systems. Lands designated as wilderness are protected from all forms of mechanization. My purpose in mentioning this, however, is not to discuss the National Wilderness Preservation System. It is to underscore that planning and management of public lands are the public's business. Public lands are important enough for the United States Senate to convene and vote in a weekend special session. United States citizens have the right to access most public lands (military lands excepted). We also have a right to express our opinion about the planning and management of these commonly-owned lands. David Rich Lewis observed:

The public lands have been and will continue to be contested space because they are public, a result of our republic which itself is a constant dance between federal and state, public and private. They represent our national birthright, the stolen heritage and dreams of others, our private possession and public trust....The ultimate contest is an individual one, to

decide whether we will continue owning the present
or begin acting for the future, for a society to match
the grandeur of our public lands. (2002, 25)

Lewis recognized that individuals must be involved in
public land planning and management, if we as a people are
to act for the future benefit of our society — for "the greatest
good [for] the greatest number in the long run" (USDA Forest
Service 2007). Over the years, federal and state land management
agencies have grown in their awareness of this fact, and they
have responded by increasing the opportunities for public
involvement. In an email to its employees, announcing a
new planning process published on December 17, 2009 in the
Federal Register, the United States Forest Service explained
that the agency's new planning [process]

offers a more strategic approach to land management
plan development, amendment, and revision. It uses
a collaborative approach to expand the public's
opportunities to be more involved in planning. [It]
establishes a *process* to dialogue with the public on
what issues are of most importance to them on a unit
of the National Forest system and to balance those
desires and needs with sound science and resource
protections. (emphasis in original)

Likewise, Georgia's Department of Natural Resources
(DNR) recognized and incorporated public input into its
Statewide Comprehensive Outdoor Recreation Plan (SCORP).

In developing the statewide plan for 2008–2013, DNR's Parks, Recreation, and Historic Sites Division "conducted seven town hall meetings across the state to give Georgians an opportunity to speak directly to state officials about the importance of outdoor recreation. The selected meeting sites — Atlanta, Brunswick, Camilla, Columbus, Milledgeville, Rome and Tallulah Falls — were within an hour's drive of most Georgians" (Georgia Department of Natural Resources 2008b, 27).

The Georgia Department of Community Affairs (DCA) is responsible for the development of a comprehensive coastal master development plan, known as the Georgia Coastal Comprehensive Plan. In 2007, DCA issued a draft stakeholder involvement plan. The plan's sole purpose was to outline public participation strategies to enhance the comprehensive planning process. The process involved surveys, a Website, and public meetings to facilitate a two-way flow of information to "ensure that all segments of the community are involved in developing a vision for the region's future" (2007, 2). In the early years of the twenty-first century, most public agencies take advantage of communications technology to increase the participation of citizens in government. This is true, as well, of public land agencies at all levels of government. As we shall see, however, this is not true of the Jekyll Island Authority.

Public lands provide ample opportunity to exercise citizenship. The public estate, after all, belongs to all citizens.

Public lands, like all public goods or services including, for example education, defense, and transportation, are held in the public trust and managed on behalf of all citizens. Unlike many public goods, however, public lands are tangible symbols of our right to freely choose our own activities, to pursue happiness through connection with natural places, and to fully participate in our government by helping to decide the future of our public lands. We are the citizen-owners of public lands. President Theodore Roosevelt, according to Daniel Filler of Yale University, considered the conservation of public lands necessary in a democratic society. This is in part because a democracy must also consider the needs of its future citizens. Roosevelt believed "that public lands and natural resources belong to the public, and that they do not exist for the unrestricted use of private industry" (Filler n.d.).

As citizen-owners, Georgians have a right to participate in the planning and management of all state parks, including Jekyll Island. Unfortunately, this right appears to have been diminished by the Jekyll Island Authority. They claim to listen, but their actions do not seem to support their claim. In 2007 and 2008, the Initiative to Protect Jekyll Island provided the Jekyll Island Authority with the written comments of over 10,000 citizens. In my assessment, the Authority's subsequent actions indicated that they had little considered the comments. This is management at odds with best practices in public land planning and management, and it is more than unfortunate that the voices of Jekyll's citizen-owners have been discounted.

Bruce Berger pointed out that:

It is an American tradition for citizens to take matters into their own hands when posterity is at stake. We have created federal agencies to manage communally held forests, open spaces, and habitats so that we may pass on our land's vitality. When agencies favor exploiters over the protection of resources, citizens seek redress in the courts and at the ballot box, for the agencies [should be] responsible to our democracy, as well as [to] the land. (2002, 33)

While Berger was speaking of federal agencies, the same can be said of state agencies. Should the citizens of Georgia continue to speak up to protect Jekyll Island for posterity? I believe the Jekyll Island situation provides an unparalleled opportunity for individual citizen action to protect a treasured public asset. As David Rich Lewis reminded us, "The ultimate contest is an individual one" (2002, 25).

Chapter 3
Putting the "Professional" in Planning

C.D., Atlanta, GA — My family and I travel to Jekyll a handful of times a year SPECIFICALLY to enjoy pristine nature, to teach our children by actually showing them the wildlife and beauty. If I wanted over-developed, traffic torture, encroachment on nature vacations, I would go to Hilton Head or St. Simons! The local wealthy families already have Amelia Island. Regular families also deserve to be able to afford to take their families to this very special and unique park.

In my undergraduate days at Virginia Tech, I was a recreation major. Really, I studied recreation. The kind you do in a local park, or as a hobby, you know, fun. People laughed when I told them I was studying recreation. They had not reflected on how important recreation is in their own lives. I refined my academic direction with my master's degree. I studied outdoor recreation. The kind of recreation you do in the great outdoors and in wilderness areas, such as canoeing, camping, and hiking. I was inspired by the thought of large areas of public land that are owned by us, the citizens.

Something one quickly learns in an outdoor recreation academic program is that the provision of publicly funded outdoor recreation is more complex than you would imagine. Like all professional fields, outdoor recreation is guided by a set of theories, principles, and what professionals call "best practices." They are called "best practices" to distinguish them from "mediocre practices" and even "worst practices." The purpose of this chapter is to briefly acquaint you with best practices in outdoor recreation. In particular, I want to introduce you to best practices in the *planning* of outdoor recreation. I want you to know this so you can compare outdoor recreation planning's best practices with the Jekyll Island Authority's planning practices over the last decade.

When you have a better understanding of how public land and outdoor recreation planning should be done, you can also better exercise your rights as a citizen-owner of public land. We are often too busy, however, to learn about our role in public land and outdoor recreation planning. Public land and outdoor recreation planning doesn't seem to be on the same level as public health concerns, education, or transportation. But it is.

Research has shown that having quality and accessible public outdoor recreation opportunities enhances physical, mental, emotional, and spiritual health. Spending time outdoors helps improve our relationships to other people and to our Earth home. Time spent outdoors in a recreational setting provides needed respite from the stresses of our fast-paced and technology-filled life. It gives us a chance to recharge. It gives perspective. It provides opportunities to learn about nature, other people, our families, and ourselves. In short, having accessible public outdoor recreation opportunities improves our quality of life. Think about your last visit to Jekyll Island, or to any state or national park or forest. Most likely, your experience was a good one, and your life was enhanced in some way by your visit. Outdoor recreation offers a *contrast* to our everyday lives. I like to think of it as re-creation, because it has that often-realized potential. These are opportunities that you would likely not want to lose.

Jekyll Island offers a true contrast to our fast-paced lives.

Preserving these opportunities, however, sometimes requires citizen action. Public lands, after all, belong to all of us. They do not belong exclusively to governors, legislators, other public officials, or to private developers; although as citizens they share our ownership of public land. In the end, it is our responsibility as a democratic society to understand, support, and become involved in the planning and management of our own publicly-held lands, otherwise we may surrender the future of these lands to others' wishes. The beauty of public lands can tempt some to try to exploit them for financial gain. This is the danger we face on Jekyll Island and other public lands today. In a letter to the editor of the *Atlanta Journal-Constitution* on November 16, 2009, Atlanta citizen Mary Shepherd noted the need for public action. In her letter, Shepherd said, "I've been following the Jekyll Island travesty since its onset, and I totally agree that something has to be done to get our island back. What I see is a groundswell in favor of doing something, but no action. Where is the petition to remove the Jekyll Island Authority and replace it with members who will better reflect the wishes of the people? Let's do it now!" In this letter, Ms. Shepherd expressed the potential transformative power of all citizen-activists.

Public Outdoor Recreation Planning

Public outdoor recreation planning is a highly developed and developing profession. On the state level, it was given a boost by the establishment of the national Land and Water Conservation Fund (LWCF). According to a history of the LWCF:

In 1958, increasing consciousness of public health and environmental issues and an expanding need for recreational space combined into a bipartisan mandate creating the Outdoor Recreation Resources Review Commission (ORRRC). After three years of research, the Commission developed specific recommendations for a national recreation program. The ORRRC report of 1961 emphasized that state and local, as well as federal, governments and the private sector were key elements in the total effort to make outdoor recreation opportunities available. (National Park Service 2009)

The ORRRC's recommendations changed the face of outdoor recreation planning in the United States and ultimately, world-wide. First, they acknowledged and documented the importance of outdoor recreation in American life. Second, they directed all recreation agencies to make the best use of available resources in light of people's needs. Important for the field of outdoor recreation planning, the recommendations were tied to a relationship between the LWCF and statewide outdoor recreation planning.

One of the ORRRC's recommendations resulted in the establishment of the LWCF. The bill creating the LWCF was passed with bipartisan support in both Houses of Congress and signed into law in 1965 (Public Law 88-578, 16 U.S.C. 460-4). The Act established a funding source for both federal acquisition of park and recreation lands and matching grants to state and local governments for recreation planning, acquisition and development. Importantly, it required statewide comprehensive outdoor recreation plans and provided a formula for allocating annual LWCF appropriations to the states and territories.

For a state to be eligible for Federal LWCF funds, a Statewide Comprehensive Outdoor Recreation Plan, or SCORP, is required. Over the years, every state has completed SCORPs on a periodic basis. Because of this legal emphasis on federal and state recreation planning tied to receiving federal funds, the field of outdoor recreation has established a high degree of professional theory and practice in planning.

Since the mid-1960s, therefore, outdoor recreation planning has become better refined. Over the years, professionals have continued to improve their planning practices. Today, there are commonly accepted best practices for outdoor recreation planning. (For example, visit the Web site of the National Association of Recreation Resource Planners, www.narrp. org, and click on "Principles of Recreation Resource Planning.") In the remainder of this chapter, we will review the accepted principles and best practices for outdoor recreation planning. Later in the chapter, we will look at Georgia's most recent

SCORP, completed in 2008.

Best Practices in Outdoor Recreation Planning

Outdoor recreation planning is closely aligned with public land planning, especially when one of the uses of public land is recreational. Over time, public agencies have learned to integrate and balance environmental and ecological concerns with recreational and other uses of public land. Professionals refer to this kind of planning as natural resource planning, to emphasize the importance of the natural amenities in planning processes and activities.

According to Hendee and Dawson (2002, 211), there are four major trends in natural resource planning:

1. The promotion of land stewardship that matches natural resources with compatible human activities. This places an emphasis first on the environmental resources, and asks which human activities are acceptable in light of these resources.

2. The protection and maintenance of natural processes that often function on a landscape scale and can extend beyond park boundaries.

3. The development of specific objectives on the basis of identified desired future environmental and social conditions. Examples include the protection or restoration of natural resources and ecosystems, plant and animal species diversity, and naturally-functioning ecosystems; and benefits such as recreation,

personal growth, and improved physical health.

4. A shift from expert planning models to a collaborative decision-making process. Past planning models relied heavily on experts and data. These planning models were often misunderstood and not accepted by the public. Today, natural resource planning is done collaboratively by the agency, users, and stakeholders of the resource. The public is engaged collaboratively, and planning professionals have established processes to enhance public participation at every stage in the planning process.

In 1997, the National Park Service outlined a planning and assessment framework to guide planning for national parks. This framework echoes the trends identified by Hendee and Dawson above. It is useful as a model for the planning of state parks as well. Elements of this framework include, but are not limited to, the following:

1. An interdisciplinary project team should be established that includes agency personnel, other agencies, stakeholders, and research institutions. A variety of professionals should be involved, such as environmental scientists, public involvement specialists, recreation specialists, geographers, social scientists, community planners, and landscape architects.

2. A public involvement strategy should be developed early in the process.

3. All planning should follow a clear statement of park purpose and historic, cultural, or environmental significance.

4. Park resources and visitor use and experience should be objectively analyzed and described. The description of visitor experience and use should be based on scientifically-based data and measurement.

5. A range of appropriate visitor experiences and environmental conditions should be identified and described. (1997, 9-11)

I like to remember these framework elements using the acronym VEE-SIPPI: Visitor Experiences, Environment, Science, Involvement, Park Purpose, and Interdisciplinary. This acronym describes much of the current best practices in professional outdoor recreation planning, and is especially appropriate to our examination of planning practices for Jekyll Island State Park.

In a later chapter, you will have the opportunity to determine whether the Jekyll Island Authority has followed VEE-SIPPI best practices for outdoor recreation planning.

Assessing Environmental and Social Impacts

When proposing a major change to an environmentally

Quality visitor experiences and preferences, as well as environmental protection, are at the heart of public land and outdoor recreation planning.

sensitive area (such as a state park), one would think that, before a decision is made, a prior assessment of the potential environmental and social impacts would be standard procedure. Congress thought so too.

For federal public lands, any proposed development or significant changes to the natural resource must be assessed under the National Environmental Policy Act (1970, PL 91-170). This act requires a thorough assessment of the environmental and social impacts of a range of proposed development or change, including the option of "no action." This is called an Environmental Impact Statement, or EIS. The public must be allowed to comment on the proposed actions. Georgia's equivalent law is the Georgia Environmental Policy Act. Unfortunately, the state's equivalent of an Environmental

Impact Statement, the Environmental Effects Report (EER), is not required by state law and carries no weight in the decision-making process. In essence, Georgia citizens have no legal tool to assess or protect the environmental and social sustainability of public lands for which development is proposed. This includes Jekyll Island. (For an EER checklist, see Appendix 2.)

The elements that encompass best practices for public land-based outdoor recreation are important. Just as one would not want a doctor, engineer, teacher, or any other professional to employ outdated practices or ignore the best practices as defined by their profession, so should we not want those planning and managing our public lands to ignore best practices.

It appears that the Jekyll Island Authority's main source for information in support of their planning process has been the Bleakly Advisory Group, a consultant firm based in Atlanta. At a public presentation on Jekyll Island in November 2008, I asked Mr. Bleakly if he had any staff members trained in professional outdoor recreation planning principles and practices. He answered that he did not. In spite of not having outdoor recreation planning expertise on staff, the Jekyll Island Authority continued to contract with the Bleakly Advisory Group to help chart the future of our state park.

Georgia Statewide Comprehensive Outdoor Recreation Plan, 2008–2013

The people of Georgia invest a fair amount of resources into the development of their Statewide Comprehensive Outdoor Recreation Plan, or SCORP. By producing a statewide plan, Georgia becomes eligible for Federal funding from the Land and Water Conservation Fund (LWCF). According to the 2008 Georgia SCORP:

In the last 40 years, Georgia has received more than $75 million from the LWCF program. Those grants have leveraged an additional $75 million from local governments through matching funds for a total of $150 million invested in outdoor recreation. Nearly 95 percent of all counties in Georgia have benefited from LWCF funding since 1965. (Georgia Department of Natural Resources 2008b, Introduction)

One of the three priorities identified by Georgia's SCORP is to conserve and properly use Georgia's natural resources.

The following comes directly from the most recent Georgia SCORP, completed in 2008:

This Statewide Comprehensive Outdoor Recreation Plan (SCORP) presents a bold agenda for outdoor recreation from 2008 to 2013. It has been crafted for two primary reasons: (1) To fulfill Georgia law mandating the development of a state policy on outdoor recreation (Georgia Code 12-3-1); and (2) To keep Georgia eligible for federal Land and Water Conservation Fund (LWCF) grant dollars.

Developing the 2008–2013 SCORP has been a true collaboration with a wide variety of allied partners. We took a multi-faceted, data-driven approach in order to fully understand the status of recreation in Georgia. Data collection consisted of:

• A comprehensive resource inventory of all federal, state, county and city outdoor recreation areas and facilities;

• Trends and benchmarks analysis of the emerging trends impacting our state;

• Statistically valid public telephone surveys to quantify opinions on outdoor recreation resources; and

• Public meetings, stakeholder groups, online comments and various other public involvement avenues for people to express their opinions. (Georgia Department of Natural Resources 2008b, 8)

It is important to note that of the four bullet points presented in the Georgia SCORP, two highlight the gathering of public input as a part of the planning process. The Georgia SCORP also noted that some of the most important trends impacting outdoor recreation in Georgia are: (1) rapid urbanization, (2) loss of greenspace, and (3) growing public support for outdoor recreation. The report also noted that in Georgia alone, over 106 acres are lost to development *every day* (8; emphasis mine). Georgia's current SCORP recommends action to stem this trend in urban development by conserving and managing areas for outdoor recreation. When considering the recent plans for further development on Georgia's barrier island state park, this question must be raised: How has the Jekyll Island Authority incorporated Georgia's SCORP recommendations into its own plans? Why is the Jekyll Island Authority pursuing development, when Georgia's SCORP recommends conservation of greenspace? After all, Jekyll Island is public land. It is a unique greenspace and a fragile ecosystem. It should, therefore, be mandatory to follow best practices in planning and management, including the integration of related publicly-funded research and planning in statewide outdoor recreation.

Further understanding of the Jekyll Island Authority's planning process will come in a later chapter. However, it is worth noting that Georgia's SCORP seems to have been ignored by the Jekyll Island Authority, despite the fact that a representative from the Georgia Department of Natural Resources sits on the Jekyll Island Authority board in an ex-officio capacity.

How can the Jekyll Island Authority discount with impunity these statewide investments in outdoor recreation planning? Surely, the Jekyll Island Authority can do a better job of planning and managing our public land for the greatest good for the greatest number in the long run, if best practices are followed.

Chapter 4
Georgia's Natural Jewel

L.H., Brunswick, GA — Some of my favorite memories from my childhood involve Jekyll Island. I learned about coastal Georgia wildlife by going to Jekyll. I remember the awestruck feeling of watching the turtles come ashore to nest and later of watching the hatchlings emerge for their first swim. I remember when sand dollars "littered" the beach and there were sea shells galore. Finding starfish was also easily done. Marsh walks were taken every year by local schoolchildren, as well as schoolchildren from further away, in order to teach us how the ecosystem within the marshes helps sustain ALL life along the coast. In order for future generations, for instance my one-month old grandson, to enjoy Georgia's Jewel the way we did, we must be ever vigilant and fight against those who seek only profit under whatever guise they employ. Jekyll is for ALL the people of Georgia to enjoy.

State parks are set aside to preserve statewide natural, historical, and cultural values. Jekyll Island is known for all of these values, and its natural environment is particularly loved by the people of Georgia. Jekyll Island is one of only four Georgia barrier islands accessible by car, and it is the only one publicly-owned and preserved as a state park. As a unique natural resource owned by the people of Georgia, a little background information is needed to understand what is at stake environmentally to the citizen-owners of Jekyll Island. Barrier islands are unique and complex ecological communities. They are found worldwide, "but are most noticeable along the east coast of North America..." (How stuff works 2009). Eight clusters of barrier islands are found in Georgia. These barrier islands, and in particular Jekyll Island, stand out from other barrier islands for a number of reasons.

Jekyll Island and St. Simons Island are the western-most of the east-coast barrier islands. If you look at a map of the United States, you will notice that Jekyll Island is almost due south of Akron, Ohio. As you look at that map, you might also notice the wide curve of the east coast, from Cape Hatteras, North Carolina to Miami, Florida. This curve is called the South Atlantic Bight. Incoming tides reach Cape Hatteras and Miami first, and there they reflect the typical ocean tidal range of two to three feet. The incoming tide funnels into the bight, gradually getting larger as it rolls towards the western-most land mass. The highest tidal ranges in the South Atlantic Bight occur at St. Simons and Jekyll Islands. David Dallmeyer, a geologist at the University of Georgia, has at times recorded a vertical-feet change of eleven feet in one day. These high tidal ranges, along with Georgia's very gradual coastal plain, allow tidal waters to extend for miles toward and into the mainland. The result is an extensive system of salt marshes, the largest on the Atlantic coast (Schoettle 1996). As you drive on the causeway to Jekyll Island, you can see some of these extensive salt marshes, especially to the south. To the uninformed, these salt marshes look like vast expanses of desolation, when in reality, salt marshes are the most biologically productive ecosystems in the world (Miller and Spoolman 2008).

The view south from the Jekyll Island causeway, showing the vast expanse of salt marsh in between Jekyll Island and the mainland.

Barrier islands are built from deposits of sand, are typically long and narrow, and usually lie parallel to the mainland coast. Barrier islands are separated by tidal inlets, areas of water that allow tidal waters to advance and recede.

Walking on Jekyll Island, one has the illusion of

permanence. Barrier islands, however, are constantly adjusting to variations in current, wave, and wind energy as well as long-term changes in sea level. It is this quality that gives them their importance as protectors of the mainland. According to University of Georgia geologist David Dallmeyer, in an email sent to me on July 26, 2009:

Waves generally approach the Georgia coast from the northeast, and wash sediment up onto a beach in a southwesterly direction. Once wave energy is expended, the sediment does not return in its original path but, instead, washes directly down the slope of the beach under the influence of gravity. This creates what's called a "long shore drift." If you're a little, tiny sand grain, and you start the morning on the north end of the beach, as these waves come up and "zigzag" you down the beach, you move. And you will end up at the end of the day further south. This is a very important process on Georgia beaches. Sand tends to move from north to south along the beaches.

North American east coast barrier islands tend to accumulate sand on their sound ends, which is indeed what is happening on Jekyll Island. Most barrier islands also accrue some sand on their northern ends, due to the movement of sand from the next barrier island lying north. Jekyll Island, however, is different. According to Taylor Schoettle, author of a field guide to Jekyll Island:

Since the dredging of the ship channel [for the Brunswick port] at the turn of the century, the erosion of most of Jekyll's [n]orth [a]rea beaches has been severe. This beach has retreated more than a thousand feet. The ship channel swallows up most of the sand drifting southward in the longshore currents from Sea Island and the other islands to the north. The sand that would normally be nourishing Jekyll's beaches is dredged out of the channel annually. (1996, 89)

This northern area has been marketed by the Jekyll Island Authority as the romantic "Driftwood Beach." In fact, it is a disturbing example of the effects of human tampering with the barrier island system. I was on Jekyll Island in December 2008, and noticed that the "Driftwood Beach" is expanding southward from the northern end of the island to the Johnson Rocks along the coast. The northern and northeastern ends of Jekyll Island are disappearing.

The Johnson Rocks (or LBJ's walls) are a seawall of sorts, constructed of large boulders called rip rap. The rip rap was placed on Jekyll Island in the mid-1960s to protect the real estate on the northern end of Jekyll Island beaches. The effect of the Johnson Rocks is clear to anyone observing the northern beach at high tide. The tide and wave energy scours the sand, lowering the beach on the ocean side of the rocks. The beach is accessible only in the hours before, during, and after low tide, and is made accessible by boardwalks over

The misnamed "Driftwood Beach" on the northern end of Jekyll Island is actually an area with the remains of trees that have fallen as a result of dredging the channel between St. Simons Island and Jekyll Island.

and the occasional paved strip through the rocks. A narrow strip of sand west of the rocks and east of the eroding dunes and forest is accessible except in severe storms, but it is a poor substitute for a true beach walk.

A 2005 National Oceanic and Atmospheric Administration (NOAA) report outlined a number of adverse impacts of coastal rip rap, including the removal or disturbance of beach habitats. When rip rap is located on a beach, a layer of hard substrate is added that can impact animal populations living on the beach. Rip rap may provide habitat for non-native species of algae, which then compete with native species of algae. Rip rap may also provide habitat for non-native species floating onto the beach from oceangoing vessels, encouraging the spread of invasive species. Finally, the NOAA report indicated that rip rap requires regular maintenance, and new rocks should be added every five to ten years because over time, the rocks will become buried by sand. Annual maintenance costs for rip rap runs between two and fifteen percent of the initial installation costs (Stamski 2005).

The Jekyll Island Authority has proposed to spend $13 million on beach renourishment at the north end of Jekyll Island. The cause of the problem, perhaps, is that the Jekyll Island Authority has not followed best practices in maintaining the Johnson Rocks since their placement. As a possible consequence, their protective function has suffered. Beach renourishment on the northern end of

During severe storms, ocean waves break over the Johnson rocks.

Jekyll is on the Authority's wish list of projects which it claims are needed and can only be financed by island redevelopment. According to Schoettle, however:

> Renourished beaches, with their sands mixed with silt and shells from the dredge spoils, are often a poor substitute for natural sand beaches. The fine silts occupy air spaces between the sand grains, smothering myriads of tiny organisms that live among the sand grains. This robs shorebirds and other animals of a valuable food source. Silty beaches often become sufficiently compact and hard as to prevent sea turtles from digging nests for a year or more after renourishment. If a natural beach does not remain in an area, then an artificial beach will not remain either, (1996, 98)

Jekyll Island is similar to other barrier islands in its ecology. During the low tides, an observer can catch a glimpse of off-shore sand bars. These off-shore sand bars often take the brunt of the incoming ocean waves. Except in times of high winds and storms, Jekyll's beaches are calm and the waves gentle as they break on the beach. Approximately twice each day, the lower beach is submerged by the high tide. Particularly on the south end, one can observe an intertidal beach with its runnels. Runnels are areas of water left on the lower beach after the tide has receded. The upper beach is only sometimes inundated by tidal waters. Along much of Jekyll's middle and southern beaches, the primary dunes remain and are protected. Behind these dunes, one can find inter-dune meadows, shrubs, and a shrub forest. These ecosystems are particularly evident on the relatively undeveloped south end of Jekyll. A maritime forest occupies much of Jekyll's inland.

Jekyll's South End

The south end of Jekyll Island is a birder's paradise. For that matter, it is also a bird's paradise. The southern beach not only provides a resting spot for numerous sea birds, its large expanse of dunes, inter-dune meadows, shrubs, and shrub forests provide a resting place for migratory birds. The Jekyll Island Banding Station, founded in 1977 and volunteer run, has provided annual banding of and data about Jekyll's migratory bird population. Many of the migratory songbirds Georgians enjoy in their own backyards have used Jekyll Island as a place to rest on their journey north and south. Over 100 species of birds have been identified at the station.

The piping plover also depends upon Jekyll Island's undisturbed shoreline. According to the U.S. Fish and Wildlife Service:

> On the south end of Jekyll Island, 1.7 miles of the
> shoreline is important enough to be designated as
> Critical Habitat for the piping plover. Although the

piping plover "winters" along the Georgia coast, it can be found here most of the year....Because of the precarious situation of these species due mainly to man's alteration of coastal habitats, further encroachment and alteration of their habitat can be detrimental. (K. Chapman 2007)

With its large expanse of undeveloped beach and dune ecosystem, the south end provides habitat for many other plant and animal species. One of the most popular of these species is the loggerhead turtle, an endangered sea turtle that depends on darkened beaches to reproduce. Wilson's plover also uses the south end of Jekyll Island for nesting.

Many birds must rest along the ocean's edge. This is a familiar scene on Jekyll's south end.

When walking along the southern shoreline, I am always thrilled by the large numbers of birds resting by the ocean's edge.

Jekyll's Maritime Forest

As a frequent visitor to Jekyll for over a decade, I somehow failed to appreciate the special character of Jekyll's maritime forest. Dr. Steve Newell, retired Director of the University of Georgia Marine Institute on Sapelo Island, introduced me to the beauty and ecological value of these forests. We discovered the rare (in Georgia) *Hibiscus grandiflorus* blooming along a freshwater maritime forest pond, rare freshwater crayfish mounds on the maritime forest floor, cabbage palms, live oaks, saw palmettos, and chain ferns lining the maritime forest trails.

Dr. Newell is particularly concerned about Jekyll Island's maritime forest wetland. In 2008, Dr. Newell wrote:

DNR Nongame Conservation personnel have characterized this wetland as "particularly important in protecting wildlife diversity" and a "significant, possibly rare natural community" that should be further investigated and documented. The NatureServe Explorer classification coming closest to this wetland is CEGL004082, Maritime Swamp Forest, but the Jekyll Island State Park swamp is unique in that it contains as dominant plants tall, aged red maples forming the canopy, and beds of two species of chain ferns on the swamp floor. Some of the red maples are three feet in diameter at breast height, and some 40 feet tall! On the floor of the swamp there are many scattered crayfish mounds, clarifying the nature of this ecosystem as a freshwater wetland. At the northern end of the swamp, there are two very large, tall bald cypress trees with knees extending out ten feet or so from the trunks. The crayfish mounds are also present under the cypress canopy, so the whole stretch of the park's swamp is indisputably a freshwater wetland.

These freshwater maritime forest wetlands are critical habitat for wildlife on Jekyll. In periods of drought, these shaded ecosystems continue to provide fresh water habitat after less protected fresh water swamps have dried up (Schoettle 1996).

A maritime forest is a delicate ecosystem. It can take centuries to restore a maritime live oak forest that has been destroyed (Schoettle 1996). In April 2009, two Georgia Department of Natural Resources biologists made an exciting discovery on Jekyll Island's south end. According to a story in the *Georgia Times-Union*:

A pileated woodpecker announced its presence last week with a ringing "kuk-kuk-kuk" in a live oak tree towering over a stand of Carolina willow and neighboring patch of wild hibiscus known as swamp rose mallow. Nearby, dragonflies flitted over fresh but tea-colored water winding through a relic dune swale, which is a low-lying, often wet stretch of land. "It's an oasis for many rare plant and animal species," said Jacob Thompson, who along with Eamonn Leonard recently discovered the previously unclassified ecological community on [Jekyll] island's southern tip. All native plants, the community of Carolina willow, swamp rose mallow and dotted smartweed create an ecosystem seldom found in the state, the Georgia Department of Natural Resources biologists said. "It's a new natural community," Leonard said. "Singularly, these plants

The wild hibiscus is a rare flower in Georgia found on Jekyll Island's south end.

are common but as a community, it's kind of rare."
The rarest plant at the site is the swamp rose mallow,
which is officially known as *hibiscus grandiflorus*, they
said. (Stepzinski 2009)

Jekyll Island also has a number of man-made fresh water
ponds. The interior, forest-lined fresh water ponds are a
haven for wildlife. I was recently introduced to Jekyll's wood
stork rookery. Wood storks are the only stork species that
breeds in North America. The rookery was not only filled
with squawking wood storks, but with an abundance of great
egrets and little green herons. Each of my photographs
revealed a forested shoreline with between eight and twenty
wading birds perched in the trees. Above me, a dozen vultures
roosted uncomfortably with me so near, shifting and grunting
their displeasure. I walked to an opening between the bushes
along the water. My view to the sides was obscured by the
thick vegetation. Standing at the water's cdge, I heard a great
"ker-plunk" about two feet away. Seconds later, an alligator
surfaced briefly in the water in front of me.

One of the island visitors' favorite wildlife experiences,
including mine, occurs on the bike path between Ben Fortson
Parkway and the entrance to Jekyll's historic district. There,
if one is lucky, an alligator can be spotted in the small pond
or sunning along its shore. I've spoken with people who
regularly ride that path in hopes of getting a glimpse of the
giant reptile.

Unlike their loggerhead relatives, the diamondback

An alligator can often be spotted sunning by the small pond beside the bike path between Ben Fortson Parkway and the Historic District.

terrapin is a relatively little known Jekyll Island turtle species. Female diamondbacks crawl out of Jekyll's tidal creeks every spring, searching for higher ground. There they will lay their eggs, if they can make it across the Jekyll causeway alive. According to the Georgia Sea Turtle Center on Jekyll, between 200 and 300 diamondbacks have been killed annually on the Jekyll causeway since they began monitoring in 2006 (Jekyll Island Authority 2009). All along the east coast, diamondbacks are in trouble. The males are killed by the thousands in crab traps, especially those set by recreational crabbers. The female population, despite road signs warning drivers, suffers under the tires of those coming to and leaving Jekyll Island. Imagine how that population of diamondback

turtles will suffer if the number of vehicles coming and
leaving Jekyll doubles in accord with the Jekyll Island
Authority's redevelopment plans.

In 2009, the Jekyll Island Sea Turtle Patrol spotted a rare
event on Jekyll's beach. The following account was written
by Jekyll resident Frank Mirasola:

> At approximately 2:30 [a.m.] Saturday, May 30
> [2009,] the Georgia Sea Turtle patrol discovered
> a leatherback turtle building a nest on the dunes
> between Blackbeard's restaurant and the convention
> center. It is the first leatherback nesting in the
> memory of most islanders and could very well be the
> first documented leatherback nesting on Jekyll Island.
> Leatherback nestings on the Georgia coast are rare;
> to date in 2009 there has been one on Sapelo Island,
> one on Sea Island, and now one on Jekyll. (Initiative
> to Protect Jekyll Island 2009b)

Adult leatherback turtles are between five and six feet
long and weigh approximately 1,000 pounds. They are the
largest of all living sea turtle species. Leatherback turtles are
an endangered species, further highlighting the importance
of Jekyll's relatively unspoiled beaches.

Jekyll Island beaches also provide habitat for loggerhead
turtle nesting. The turtle nesting season begins in May and
lasts through October. Sea turtle nesting, which occurs at
night, is disrupted by artificial lighting. According to

Escambia County (Florida) Extension Service Web site:

> It takes hatchlings two to three days to dig out of the
> nest. They usually dig and emerge as a group. Once at
> the surface, hatchlings orient to the brightest horizon
> to find the ocean. Unfortunately, artificial lights often
> confuse hatchlings and result in hatchlings crawling
> inland, away from the water. These hatchlings are eaten
> by predators, run over by cars, or killed by the heat of
> the sun the following day. It is believed that only one in
> 1,000 hatchlings survives to adulthood. (2009)

In 2008, Jekyll residents Dr. Steve Newell and Bonnie Newell began work to propose a modern beach lighting ordinance for Jekyll Island. After months of research and communication with the Jekyll Island Authority, a modern beach lighting ordinance was adopted. This ordinance specifies how lighting may be used near the beach during turtle nesting season. For example, no light source or reflection from a light source may be visible from the beach. This ordinance was a critical step in protecting the sea turtle nesting habitat on Jekyll. A link to the Jekyll Island Authority Beach Lighting Ordinance is available in Chapter 15.

Unfortunately, the adoption of the ordinance did not mean that it would be consistently enforced. At the start of the 2009 turtle nesting season, the Newells discovered three violations of the lighting ordinance. When they brought these violations to the attention of the Jekyll Island Authority, two of the offending lights were extinguished. The third and most damaging of the lights was shining onto the beach at the Days Inn. The Newells contacted hotel management to no avail. After repeated attempts, they climbed the corporate ladder, finally reaching the green division of Wyndham Worldwide. Soon thereafter, the Days Inn manager sent an email to the Newells, informing them that the light was fixed, and that the Days Inn has always had respect for loggerhead turtles.

Climate Change and Jekyll Island

On August 2, 2008, www.weather.com produced a short video for their series "Forecast Earth." This video, called "Where did the beaches go?" was about climate change and Jekyll Island. Host Natalie Allen interviewed Emory University Ecologist Dr. Tony Martin, who reported that scientists have "very reliable evidence" that Jekyll Island is changing "in accordance with climate change." According to the United Nations, sea level may rise between seven and twenty-three inches in this century. If that happens, Jekyll's beach will be completely underwater. Martin noted the tendency for southeastern storms to be "more frequent and with greater intensity" than in the past. Allen also interviewed [Jekyll Island Authority private partner and developer] Linger Longer Communities' Jim Langford (now retired), who emphasized that Linger Longer's plan was based on science. Langford also claimed that Linger Longer would be using state-of-the-art environmental building practices to mitigate environmental concerns. In a public forum about Jekyll Island held in Atlanta in 2007, I asked Mr. Langford to quote the scientific sources used to determine the environmental soundness of the Linger Longer plan. He had no answer.

Jekyll Island Conservation Plan

The 2004 Jekyll Island Master Plan noted the importance of crafting a conservation plan as a guiding document. The introduction to the plan recognized the critical nature of Jekyll Island's environment:

> As noted, Jekyll Island's first and foremost amenity is its natural environment and island ecology. To complement the development plan recommended in this master plan update, we recommend the Jekyll Island Authority initiate a conservation plan for the island soon after the development plan process has begun. This conservation plan should provide an in-depth examination of Jekyll's flora and fauna and identify the critical issues and impacts development and redevelopment of the island can have on the island's ecology. (Robert Charles Lesser 2004, 3)

The Jekyll Island Authority contracted with a consultant to draft this conservation plan for the island. This plan was produced in 2007 by Cabin Bluff Land Management. Part 1 is a nicely produced listing (with photos) of the flora and fauna that should be found on Jekyll Island. Part 2 contains environmental concerns and management recommendations for natural areas on Jekyll Island.

The draft conservation plan, according to public reaction, did not go far enough in its analysis of the likely impacts of further island development. Revisions were made to the plan but were subsequently modified by the Jekyll Island Authority. When questions were raised about why the plan's revisions had been rejected, the document was turned over to Georgia Assistant Attorney General George Zier for review.

The Jekyll Island Conservation Plan sat on counselor George Zier's desk from November 2007, awaiting review and official release. After the conservation plan was sent to the Attorney General's office for review, there was little mention of the plan at board meetings for months. Meanwhile, the push for development was moving forward and concern over the absence of a plan to guide development was growing among Jekyll's friends. Members of the public began regularly asking the Authority board for an update on the progress of the legal review. Below are some excerpts from the notes of Jekyll Island Authority board meetings, kept by Dr. Steve Newell, dealing with the conservation plan and when it would be returned to the Authority by Assistant Attorney General George Zier.

- June 14, 2008
  Counsel Zier indicated only a couple of chapters are left to review, so the conservation plan should be ready for adoption by the end of July.

- August 11, 2008
  Counsel Zier had estimated that he would have the plan ready for the board at the September, 2008, meeting.

- September 15, 2008
  Chairman Ben Porter asked Counsel Zier to speak to the status of the Jekyll Island State Park conservation plan. Zier reported that he is still working on the plan, but expects to have it ready for presentation at the next board meeting. Board member Becky Kelley asked for clarification — will the conservation plan be ready for the next (October) board meeting? Answer: That is the target date.

- October 20, 2008
  Counsel George Zier has now been encumbered with any number of legal issues, and his responsibilities have had to be prioritized. The conservation plan is still on his desk, and no commitments can now be made as to the date of its release. After some other legal issues are resolved, the plan will be high on the board's list of priorities.

- November 10, 2008
  Bob Krueger shut off questions regarding the park's conservation plan by asserting that it is not available yet. He stated that it is still working forward, but it is taking a back seat at this point.

- December 15, 2008
  George Zier responded on the phone, stating that he now has contract details to work out, so he won't be getting back to the plan until January. Mindy Egan restated her position that adoption of the conservation plan should have been a prerequisite (not an afterthought) to firming up plans for real-estate development in the park. She wondered how the delaying of the plan's adoption squares with the Authority's many assertions regarding its desire to protect the park's natural ecosystems. Krueger stated that he did not see why the plan should be adopted before the private-partner contract was prepared and signed. He felt that the revitalization goals can be met with or without the conservation plan, and the natural resources can still be protected.

- 14 January, 2009
  The earliest date upon which legal review of the conservation plan can continue is 9 February, and the Authority has not yet determined the extent of review that they will require, so a date for submission of the reviewed plan to the Authority cannot now be projected.

- April 20, 2009

  Chairman Krueger noted that Assistant Attorney General Zier has a number of things going on. He observed that issues get prioritized, and the conservation plan has been repeatedly pushed down on the priority list.

- August 10, 2009

  Mindy Egan reported to the Jekyll Island Authority Board that "this day marks the 636th day since the board sent the conservation plan to the Attorney General's office for review."

In an undated essay, the Center for a Sustainable Coast's Executive Director David Kyler noted:

A conservation plan begun years ago was never completed and has been effectively impounded at the attorney general's office for more than a year. The proposed development prepared under the Jekyll Island Authority's "guidance" by Linger Longer Communities has not had the benefit of being informed by professional assessment of wildlife habitat, threatened and endangered species, and other basic concepts of responsible conservation.

At the September 14, 2009 Jekyll Island Authority board meeting, after a delay of nearly two years, the board recommended that counselor Zier return the conservation plan to the Authority with some suggestions on how to move forward with a review of the plan. Jekyll Island Authority Executive Director Jones Hooks suggested that a team of environmental experts, including people from the DNR, Nature Conservancy, and Georgia Conservancy, would be assembled to review and revise the plan. Revisions would be addressed at a public hearing prior to board adoption. He estimated it would take one year to complete this task.

Clearly, a reworked conservation plan will not be ready in time to guide plans for development of the seventeen-acre area along the beach that includes a retail center, two hotels, condominiums, and timeshares. Plans for two other hotel redevelopment projects may also be completed before the conservation plan is finalized.

To me, with the specter of more development coming to Jekyll Island, and much of it along the primary dunes, it is irresponsible of the Jekyll Island Authority to move forward without the benefit of environmental assessments and a conservation plan. The long-impounded draft plan, completed in 2007 by Cabin Bluff Management, enumerates the following rare, threatened, and endangered species on Jekyll:

- Threatened plant species: 2
- Rare plant species: 1
- Endangered fish species: 1
- Threatened reptile species: 2
- Endangered reptile species: 3

- Unusual reptile species: 1
- Endangered bird species: 2
- Threatened bird species: 3
- Rare bird species: 5
- Endangered mammal species: 3
  (2007, J-53)

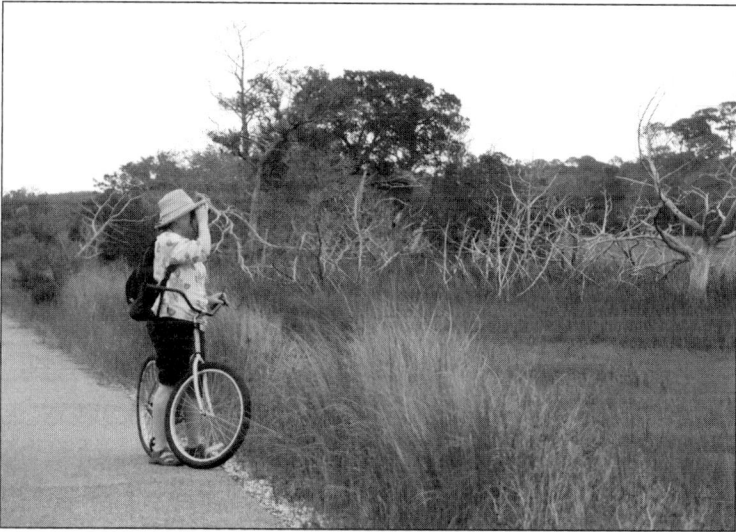

Jekyll Island is known for its superb birding opportunities.

The first paragraph of the Cabin Bluff conservation plan summary highlights the value and importance of Jekyll's environment:

The natural values present on Jekyll Island are one of its biggest attractions for tourists, residents, and businesses. Conserving and enhancing those values

as development and redevelopment pressures rise is a
critical step in insuring that Jekyll Island is available
for future generations. (Cabin Bluff Management
2007, L-48)

Besides the two-year impoundment of the conservation
plan, the Jekyll Island Authority has failed to assess the
environmental impacts of its development plans. In essence,
there are no scientifically-credible environmental assessments
or recommendations being used in the planning, management,
and development of Jekyll Island State Park.

The U.S. Fish and Wildlife Service, in a public comment
session held on November 14, 2007 on Jekyll Island, noted that:

There appears to be a net loss of wildlife habitat from
Linger Longer [hotel, retail, and residential] plans as
opposed to replacing outdated motels, as was originally
planned. Many of the parks appear to be turf grass
and palm trees and hardscape interspersed among the
buildings. These areas will have little value for wildlife,
particularly thousands of migratory birds, which use the
Georgia coast as a migratory pathway between nesting
and wintering grounds. Because of the large scale of
this proposed development and the subsequent increase
in human population of Jekyll Island, certain wildlife
species will need to be controlled to accommodate the
increased human population on the island. It does not
appear in the plans that a carrying capacity for humans

or wildlife populations has been determined for Jekyll Island. An island has a limited supply of necessary resources to support life. (K. Chapman 2007)

Environmentally-Sensitive Development?

The initial development plan submitted by Linger Longer Communities, then the Jekyll Island Authority's private sector partner, was widely opposed by the public. This was primarily for its encroachment upon the public beach area north of Jekyll's convention center. It eventually became clear that this site was also within the shore protection zone as governed by Georgia's Shore Protection Act (O.G.C.A. 2-5-230, et seq.). Linger Longer withdrew the plan and developed a new one located south of the convention center, but not until after a year-long campaign by Linger Longer and the Jekyll Island Authority to argue that the plan was something Jekyll needed and Georgians wanted. The irony of the initial plan's placement in the shore protection zone was Linger Longer's assertion of how environmentally-sensitive their plans were. On January 31, 2008, I attended a public input session in Atlanta. There, Linger Longer's Jim Langford (now retired) emphasized the importance of environmentally-sensitive development. The Linger Longer development would, he boasted, be LEED (Leadership in Energy and Environmental Design) certified, and it would become the first coastal EarthCraft community. (EarthCraft is a green building program.) For the second time, I asked Mr. Langford how Linger Longer could place a large commercial and residential development up against primary dunes and call it environmentally-friendly. I also asked him to identify the science that supported their development plans. Once again, he had no answer.

Unfortunately for those of us who care about environmentally-sensitive design, we heard no more boasting about environmental commitment from Linger Longer Communities. Instead, as Assistant Attorney George Zier noted in a November 26, 2008 letter to Jekyll Island Authority Chairman Bob Krueger, "[Linger Longer] has *not* agreed to either work toward or attain any environmental certification or standard, such as the LEED, EarthCraft, Energy Star, or similar standards." (emphasis in original)

Summary

Jekyll Island's environment, like all relatively undeveloped southeastern United States barrier islands, is special. It is special for its dramatic and lovely landscapes and rich wildlife habitat, its beautiful beaches, dunes, and marsh landscapes. It is special for its variety of barrier island ecosystems. It is also special because of its protective function. Southeastern barrier islands formed over thousands of years, and since their formation, have protected the North American southeastern coast from ocean storms. Jekyll Island is only one of four Georgia barrier islands accessible to the public by vehicle and is, at this writing, also the most natural of the four. Jekyll Island offers the most accessible opportunity in Georgia for visitors to experience natural barrier island ecology.

Chapter 5
Jekyll Island State Park: The First 50 Years

D.P., Acworth, GA — Jekyll Island should remain a place for the citizens of Georgia (as well as other visitors) to visit without the commercialism that is seen at other places. I enjoy the natural atmosphere where we can enjoy the beaches and safely bike rides. Jekyll Island has changed very little in the over thirty years I have been coming. The relaxing atmosphere is what keeps bringing me back. Don't let the developers ruin the island! Once it is gone, it will be gone forever.

In 1947, the State of Georgia ordered condemnation proceedings to begin so that Jekyll Island could be purchased for the development of a "great public beach park" (Bagwell 2001, 21). The island was purchased from the Jekyll Island Club, a group of wealthy entrepreneurs from the northern United States who had owned the island since 1881. The man responsible for promoting the acquisition of Jekyll Island for the people of Georgia was State Revenue Commissioner M.E. Thompson. Thompson later became governor, and it was under his administration in 1947 that Jekyll Island was purchased. The state park was officially opened in 1948.

Thompson envisioned Jekyll Island as a state park for the "plain people of Georgia." According to Martin and McCash:

> The state took possession of Jekyll Island on October 7, 1947, thus ending Jekyll's period of splendid isolation as a millionaires' retreat and beginning its era as a state park for the masses. This transaction was symbolic of larger post-war changes in southern tourism. Not only does it reflect the democratization of tourism and the rapid rise of middle-class resorts, it also illustrates the increased role of state governments in promoting and financing the growth of tourism after World War II. (2003,163)

The Eatonton, Georgia *Messenger* reported on October 30, 1947:

> Jekyll Island might have been a "rich man's paradise" in the past, but such will be far from the case when the state of Georgia officially begins operations of the famous coastal resort as a state park January 1, state park Director Charlie Morgan revealed Saturday.

> "We're going to turn Jekyll into a paradise for the average Georgia citizen," said Morgan, who recently returned from an inspection tour of the state's newly acquired territory on the Georgia coast near Brunswick. Morgan said a scale of prices in keeping

with those now prevailing at the nineteen other parks in the Georgia system would be put into effect at the island park soon after the state opens Jekyll to the public early next year. "The chief purpose in acquiring Jekyll was to provide a beach park for all the people of Georgia," said Morgan.

Without convenient automobile access to the island, tourism did not take off as was hoped. Thompson's successor, Herman Talmadge did not support the idea of state ownership of Jekyll Island. Therefore, in 1949, Talmadge leased the island's facilities to private enterprise for the remainder of his term, and he requested that state legislators create a Jekyll Island State Park Authority to administer the leases.

Established in February 1950, the Jekyll Island Authority...is a quasi-public corporation that has broad powers to develop, administer, and promote the island as a tourist attraction. Consisting originally of five members appointed by Governor Talmadge, the Authority was obligated by its charter to permit development on "not more than one-half of the land area of Jekyll Island, which lies above water at mean high tide," and to create a vacation spot "at the lowest rates reasonable and possible for the benefit of the people of Georgia. (Martin and

McCash 2003, 64.)

Calling for the operation of the public facilities of the park "at the lowest rates reasonable and possible for the benefit of the ordinary people of the State of Georgia," the Jekyll Island State Park Authority Act (Law Number 630, 1950, section 7) left no room for doubt. Jekyll Island was to be the people's park.

One of the early Jekyll Island Authority board members was J.D. Compton, who carefully and with integrity sought to plan and manage Jekyll Island State Park. It was he who insisted on keeping Jekyll Island accessible to all Georgians. Compton was largely responsible for the hiring of Atlanta Engineering firm Robert and Company, Associates. Andrew Steiner, the chief architect of Jekyll Island, was responsible for the design's emphasis on Jekyll's natural amenities. He kept two-thirds of the island undeveloped, preserving for future option one of Jekyll's most treasured characteristics.

In the early 1950s, Jekyll Island's current situation was foreshadowed by an increasing number of questionable deals. The story is best told by Martin and McCash (2003):

As the Jekyll Island Authority [JIA] began implementation of its plan, Georgia politics entered the picture once again, ushering in a troubled period of what many journalists judged to be corruption and political favoritism. In January 1954, the State Highway Department awarded a $207,893 paving contract for the Jekyll Island causeway to Acme Construction Company owned by State senator James ("Jimmy") Dykes from Cochran, Georgia. Dykes was also reportedly a good friend of Governor Herman Talmadge, future governor Marvin Griffin, State Highway Chairman James Gillis, and JIA Chairman D.B. Blalock, who himself owned two businesses that sold road paving equipment. These political connections were vital in Dykes's ultimate control, direct or indirect, of almost all business activities on the island.

After the Jekyll Creek Bridge finally opened on December 11, 1954, Dykes's influence grew rapidly. By the end of 1955, he had acquired exclusive leases on paving projects, building supplies, hotel properties, concessions, a gas station, and general contracting. In fairness to Dykes, he was sometimes the only bidder on the various projects. On the other hand, he clearly had an advantage in that he often had prior knowledge about the call for bids, which, after the posting in newspaper announcements, usually gave bidders only two weeks to submit. Ever since he had acquired the lease to open the island's first business, the Bonded Building and Supply Company, he had the additional financial advantage of having crew and materials already on the island. As a consequence, for a time Dykes would have a virtual monopoly on the construction and contracting business on Jekyll.

In late May 1955, the Authority leased the Jekyll Island Clubhouse as a hotel to a firm from Cochran, Georgia, after Dykes had assured JIA that he had no connection with the company. After the lease was granted, however, it was revealed that, not only was Dykes a principal stockholder, he was also designated as the operator of the Jekyll property. Although JIA chair Sen. D.B. Blalock insisted that "it was two months before we ever had any inkling that Jimmy was connected with it," he seems to have benefited financially as well from Dykes's operations. An audit in 1955 showed that Blalock's firms had sold more than $85,000 worth of road building machinery and parts to the state for use at Jekyll. It also revealed that Dykes was in arrears in the rent on his leased properties. Even after these conflicts of interest and lease violations were discovered, the Authority negotiated an additional $218,000 paving contract with Dykes and his brother-in-law and allowed him to open the Jekyll Insurance Corporation, which also dealt in real estate and cottage rentals on the island.

These shady dealings did not go unnoticed. Jim Compton, who oversaw JIA purchases, began to question requisitions and invoices related to Dykes. On June 17, 1955, he complained to Blalock that "I am opposed to the very sloppy way in which materials and equipment are being ordered...I don't think anyone can tell what has been ordered, what it cost, and who authorized the [purchase]. I do not care to be involved in the controversy which is very likely to arise over the placing and payment of these orders." Six weeks later, on July 30, Compton stunned Authority members by tendering his resignation, ostensibly for reasons that "have to do with my business and my health." However, in a private letter to Blalock, he begged: "Please don't let any one individual or group get control of all the island's best facilities, as has been the tendency during the past eight to ten months, for it will hurt the further development of the island and bring great criticism down on the authority."

Compton's words were prophetic, for within a few weeks of his resignation, the state's Legislative Economy Committee launched an investigation of the Jekyll Island Authority. The committee's controversial hearings resulted in a 78-page report that severely criticized the Authority for sloppy bookkeeping and recommended dissolving JIA and turning the island over to [Georgia's] parks department or selling it altogether. This report was released amid an avalanche of criticism from politicians and journalists, directed at the high prices at Jekyll Island and the Authority's policy of leasing residential lots. Throughout the mid-

1950s, many people complained that the cost for accommodations at Jekyll "is far out of reach of the average Georgian" and urged the Authority to build low-cost housing and motels "so the average man could take his family there for a summer vacation."

More importantly, the residential leasing policy came under heavy scrutiny after lessees had difficulties securing mortgage loans on leased property and a Georgia Supreme Court ruling apparently cleared the way for Glynn County to tax Jekyll properties. Asserting that the leasing policy inhibited development of the island, some legislators viewed it as "out of step with the way America does things" by putting the state in competition with private developers. Governor Marvin Griffin, asserting "I'm a free enterprise man myself," indicated he was in favor of selling residential lots outright or perhaps swapping the entire island for a nuclear reactor. To study the matter, he created a special legislative commission, which recommended that the state keep Jekyll Island as a state park and even spend another $397,731, most of it earmarked for properties leased by Jimmy Dykes. Governor Griffin acquiesced to the committee's recommendations, and the controversy over Jekyll Island temporarily waned.

However, in July 1956, shortly after the opening of the $10 million bridge linking the Jekyll causeway to Brunswick, all hell broke loose. First, Dykes was accused of selling beer on the island without a liquor license; then the *Atlanta Constitution* published a series of scathing articles that charged the Authority with corruption. In response, Griffin announced that he wanted "to dispose of this 'white elephant'," and he froze all further spending on Jekyll. In the wake of such publicity, tourists flocked to the island "to see what the ruckus was all about," but overall they were pleasantly surprised by what they found. One Atlanta visitor commented: "I went down expecting, from newspaper reports, to find a jumble of inefficiency and beer joints, but I found neither... In fact, I have never seen a more beautiful, natural or better-run place." Nonetheless, after nearly a year of negative publicity, there was still strong sentiment to shake up the Authority or sell the island. In the legislature, a compromise emerged that rejected the notion of selling Jekyll and instead created a new Authority comprised of high-ranking officials, including the Secretary of State, the public service commissioner, the state auditor, the attorney general, and the Director of the Department of State Parks. (Martin and McCash 2003, 166-168, reprinted with permission of the University of Alabama Press.)

Jekyll Island was not immune to the civil rights issues

troubling the nation. The south end of Jekyll was developed for African-Americans, but these facilities were never equal to other facilities in quality. In the mid-1960s, Jekyll Island integrated peacefully, following a class-action suit against the Jekyll Island Authority by the state and local NAACP. This suit was resolved by a ruling in favor of desegregation. The Dolphin Hotel, developed as the African American hotel on Jekyll, eventually became the 4-H Center. Today, the 4-H Center annually introduces thousands of Georgia students to coastal ecology (Martin and McCash 2003).

In 1983, the University of Georgia's Institute for Community and Area Development (ICAD) produced a Comprehensive Land Use Plan for the Jekyll Island Authority. The report stated that, in making recommendations, "the most pertinent of these policy decisions is the set of goals adopted by the Authority in 1982:

- Maintain and protect the island resources using funds generated from its amenities;

- Actively solicit visitors from all income levels, but primarily those with average incomes;

- Beautify the island through conservation of resources and additional plantings;

- Construct or reconstruct aesthetically-pleasing facilities; and

- Advertise the island's beauty.

Further, ICAD recommended, among other things, that

the Authority adopt the following (emphasis in original):

- All land use must conform to and respect the special nature of a coastal barrier island;

- Land use should reflect the image of Jekyll Island as a natural island with a rich historic heritage, to which tasteful and appropriate accommodations have been made for human physical and recreational needs;

The report also stated that "a linear belt of land lying along the beach shall be classified as a 'zone of no encroachment.' This zone is to be left in a natural state or restored to its natural state. No new development along the beach will be permitted." As we will see, these recommendations appear to have been ignored in the development planning in the first decade of the 21st century, and especially the recommendation calling for no new beachside development.

I also discovered, while reading the ICAD Comprehensive Land Use Plan, that the Jekyll Island Authority had commissioned another study, this one in 1981. This study, done by Hammer, Siler, George Associates, included a market analysis which was apparently aimed at increasing visitation to the island. This study must have been done as a follow up to decline in visitation experienced in the 1970s, a time when rampant inflation and tight gasoline supplies crippled the nation.

In 1982, the year before the ICAD study was completed, the Jekyll Island Authority produced a "Fact Sheet" on the status of Jekyll Island. The Fact Sheet noted that, in 1977, the Governor and Legislature called for a change in the direction of Jekyll Island's management. The reasons for this change included a decline in tourism on Jekyll Island with resulting hotel and restaurant closures. In response, the Jekyll Island Authority was restructured to seven members, four of whom were citizens from around the state. The other three included the Lt. Governor, the Secretary of State, and the Commissioner of the Department of Natural Resources.

Why did the Governor and the General Assembly recommend these structural changes? A hint may be found in a letter sent on March 30, 1977 from then-Department of Natural Resources Commissioner Joe D. Tanner to Governor Busbee. In this letter, he said:

> There continue to be major problems at Jekyll Island and I am personally not satisfied with the way these problems are being handled. As a matter of fact, little or no effort is being made to resolve most of the problems. I believe it is essential for this Department and the Office of Planning and Budget to work together with the Authority to begin addressing some of these problems and to propose solutions before we are embarrassed by the press and before the legislature takes the matter into its own hands.

This letter from Joe Tanner requested a change from a board consisting of high ranking public officials to one partially consisting of appointed members. It represents the beginning of the return to the initial Authority board structure. That structure spawned corruption in the late 1950s, with no-bid contracts given repeatedly to Jimmy Dykes. It was public outcry against this rampant corruption that caused the board structure to be changed in the late 1950s to one of "high ranking officials," rather than appointed members. In 1977, the changes to the Jekyll Island Authority board structure spurred by Tanner's letter provided the first step in the direction of the current board structure. Today, the Jekyll Island Authority board is appointed by the governor, with a seat for an ex-officio member from the Department of Natural Resources. This lowers its accountability to Georgia citizens and can reduce legislative intent. According to the Morris News Service:

> The General Assembly may pass the legislation and the governor may sign them into law, but it's the boards of agencies and commissions that interpret the laws and enact rules that determine the laws' details. A board that doesn't favor a law can water down the rules about it to such an extent as to make the law meaningless. Or the rules can be more restrictive than the legislators or governor intended. (Jones 2009b)

Joe Tanner eventually left the Department of Natural Resources, but he did not leave the Jekyll Island issue. In 2008 and 2009, he was a Georgia lobbyist. His primary client was

Linger Longer Communities, the corporation selected by the Jekyll Island Authority board to be its private partner on Jekyll Island. Interestingly, one of the principals in Linger Longer Communities, Jamie Reynolds, served on the Department of Natural Resources Advisory Board from 1997 until 2001, his term overlapping with the term of Commissioner Joe Tanner. In 1981, the Jekyll Island Authority requested and received permission to charge user fees, similar to Lake Lanier Islands and Stone Mountain Memorial Park. Without such fees, the Authority claimed it would be bankrupt within two years. In 1982, the Jekyll Island Authority reported that "for the first time since being bought by the state, the Authority has paid all its operating expenses and equipment purchases from its own revenues generated from island visitors and has about a four percent surplus" (Jekyll Island State Park Authority 1982).

For the island's first thirty-four years, its financial management had not been self-sufficient. In the 1980s, the Jekyll Island Authority began making capital improvements to the island "to insure self-sufficiency." These projects included, for example, restoration of the Jekyll Island Club, a "Wharf, Aquarama, bike paths, parking lots, dune crossings, nature trail boardwalks," and the renovation of the Dolphin Hotel for a 4-H camp (Jekyll Island Fact Sheet 1982). While most of these facilities are still standing, the Aquarama is conspicuously absent from Jekyll Island.

The following text was written by Dory Ingram, Atlanta Metro Coordinator of the Initiative to Protect Jekyll Island,

and sent to me via email on March 3, 2009:

Whatever became of the Jekyll Island State Park Aquarama? The recreational facility was originally built in the 1960s, and between 1981 and 1983, the Jekyll Island Authority applied for and received Federal Land and Water Conservation Fund (LWCF) dollars in the amount of $112,000 to refurbish the pool and construct support facilities and trails just south of the Convention Center, where the pool was located. Known as the Aquarama, the site was a popular spot for local and out-of-state visitors, who paid a nominal fee to help with maintenance of the pool. Now the pool is gone and only an empty lot remains.

The Land and Water Conservation Act of 1965 stipulates that a recreational facility acquired or developed with LWCF assistance must be maintained in reasonable repair by the local project sponsor throughout its lifetime to prevent undue deterioration and to encourage public use. The law further stipulates that a posted LWCF acknowledgment sign must be displayed at the project site so that the public is aware that the facility has been developed with their tax dollars. The funding for the Aquarama was accepted from the U.S. National Park Service, Department of the Interior, with an understanding of, and in agreement with, those terms.

Documentation obtained through the Georgia Open Records Act reveals that throughout the life of the pool, the Jekyll Island Authority was cited several times during inspections for failure to display the LWCF signage. Further, the pool was allowed to fall into disrepair despite the stewardship requirements of the grant, until a decision was made by the Authority in 1992 to demolish the pool and replace it with an empty lot. This lot is the future site of [the planned timeshares] development.

In the latter part of the 1960s, the Jekyll Island Authority had begun to consider how to reach self-sufficiency. One of their solutions was to approve the construction of Sea Circus on Jekyll's south end in 1970. Sea Circus was to be a smaller version of Sea World. Opposition to Sea Circus was led by Jekyll resident Si Fryer (Martin and McCash 2003).

This controversy was the impetus for State Representative Mike Egan to introduce House Bill 473, which when enacted into law in 1971 became known as the Mike Egan law. This law prohibited the Jekyll Island Authority from developing "more than thirty-five percent of the land area of Jekyll Island which lies above water at mean high tide" (Law Number 427, 1971).

Martin and McCash noted, however, that the Mike Egan law did not define development. This omission created an opportunity for the Jekyll Island Authority. The Authority argued that golf courses were not really development, but were, in fact, habitat for wildlife. In 1995, the Authority began constructing a golf course without obtaining the necessary permits, and island residents and area environmentalists protested under the leadership of Jean and Leonard Poleszak. The Georgia Environmental Protection Division halted the development of the golf course. Shortly thereafter, the Jekyll Island Authority executive director and board chairman resigned. Legislation was passed that required a new master plan to guide Jekyll's future. In an ironic twist, considering the events of the early 21st century, Governor Zell Miller claimed as he signed the bill into law, "...we are not going to ever overdevelop this environmentally sensitive island" (Martin and McCash 2003, 175).

According to Martin and McCash, the next thirty years of Jekyll Island history focused attention on natural and historic preservation. In December 1986, the newly restored Jekyll Island Club opened for visitors. Renewing the historic district has been a priority for the Jekyll Island Authority. The Georgia Sea Turtle Center, opened in 2007, is the newest building to be renovated in the historic district.

In 1996, the Jekyll Island Authority published a master plan for Jekyll's future. This master plan initiated Jekyll Island's most recent history.

The historic district offers an historic and cultural experience to Jekyll Island visitors.

Chapter 6
"Gold Rush" on Jekyll Island

M.M., Atlanta, GA — For forty five years, Jekyll Island has been a refuge for me and my family. Year after year, its solitude and undeveloped beauty, especially in the winter months, has restored my equanimity and peace of mind. I abhor the development along most of the southeast coast, yet I understand that many folks find that appealing. I do not. But as long as Jekyll remains much as it is, I have an affordable place to go to meet my needs. Of course, the aging motels need redevelopment. That needs to be done in a way that maintains the low-key and financially accessible ocean front accommodations that are Jekyll's legacy.

The Jekyll Island Authority is responsible for the island's planning and management. The Authority is under the direction of a board of directors which, since the 1980s, has been appointed by Georgia's governor. The way in which the appointed Jekyll Island Authority of the 21st century appears to discount public opinion, deflect public scrutiny, and act with impunity may to be related to its accountability to Georgia's governor. Elected boards, or those with elected officials must, alternatively, be primarily accountable to the public who elects them.

Like most Jekyll Island visitors, I never thought about the Jekyll Island Authority board. I had no idea how much power it had to radically change the state park character of Jekyll Island. I thought Jekyll Island would always be just what it was. In 2004, I heard a rumor while vacationing on the island. A local shop owner in the historic district told me that big changes were on the horizon. Governor Perdue and the Jekyll Island Authority would begin a huge development project and nothing would be the same on the island. He was leaving before it happened, because he could not stand to see Jekyll Island ruined. He was not in his shop the next year. As he had promised, he sold his shop and left.

In March 2006, I was again on the island, lodging at the Buccaneer Hotel. My husband and I had heard the news — the Buccaneer would be demolished within a year or two. The hotel staff, resigned to the hotel's demise, provided mediocre service. "Why bother?" they implied. Two days before we were to return home, I opened my almost-week-old copy of the *Athens Banner-Herald* newspaper, which I had hurriedly stuffed into my bag as we left for our vacation. There, ominously positioned on the obituary page, was a story about the upcoming development of Jekyll Island. I recalled my conversation with the shop owner in 2004. I read that David Egan, a Jekyll resident, was opposed to the development plan. I looked him up, and within the hour we met at Jekyll's small retail area, near the post office, all of us straddling our bicycles. David and Mindy Egan confirmed the disturbing rumors: Jekyll Island was slated for extensive development.

I did not know at the time what had happened to bring the specter of additional hotel, retail, condominium, and timeshare development to Jekyll Island. I still do not know the entire history, but I will share as much as I know. If you have questions, the best source of information is the Jekyll Island Authority. You may, however, need to become proficient at making Georgia Open Records Act (GORA) requests. (See Appendix 3 for a template.)

The 1996 Master Plan

In 1996, the Jekyll Island Authority adopted a master plan for the island. For whatever reasons, the Jekyll Island Authority did not seem to coordinate Jekyll's planning with the Georgia Statewide Comprehensive Outdoor Recreation Plan (SCORP). (For a description of Georgia's SCORP, see Chapter 3.) The objectives of the Jekyll Island Master Plan were:

1. Development of management strategies to enhance and/or continue successful operation of commercially leased operations.

2. Evaluation and recommendations regarding Authority-controlled operations as to upgrades, capital improvements, effectiveness of product delivery, or possible privatization of these operations.

3. Incorporation of the Historic District Master Plan, completed in October 1995.

4. Recommendations for the protection of unimproved areas, with respect to access, nature experience, interpretation, and educational opportunities that are not disruptive and are consistent with remaining unimproved. "A balance is sought in preserving the natural setting, while serving as a classroom of the barrier, coastal island environment easily accessible by the general public." [Quotes in original.]

5. Allowance and consideration of input from a broad cross-section of interest groups, residents, business owners, and conservation organizations.

The Jekyll Island Authority seems keen to meet objectives 1–3. As for objective 4, the Authority has chosen to proceed with major development and redevelopment projects without environmental assessments or an approved conservation plan. This is the case, even though the planned development projects would result in greater infrastructure and environmental impact on the island. What makes this even more incredible is that a draft conservation plan was developed in 2007 by Cabin Bluff Management, a private contractor, at the request of the Jekyll Island Authority. The plan's adoption and distribution was delayed for nearly two years after citizens and environmental groups took issue with some of its components. As described in Chapter 4, as of October 2009 the plan was still collecting dust on Georgia Assistant Attorney George Zier's desk, apparently too late to guide development of the planned beachfront construction. As for objective 5, the Jekyll Island Authority seems to have discounted input from "a broad cross-section of interest groups," including citizens, residents, and conservation organizations.

Is Jekyll Island Already Over the Development Cap?

One of the most critical findings of the 1996 Master Plan was that Jekyll Island was 32.44 percent developed. By law (Georgia code 12-3-243, otherwise known as the Mike Egan law), Jekyll Island must remain 65 percent undeveloped. The Jekyll Island Authority determined that 2.56 percent more of the Island could be developed, equaling 108.35 acres.

The fluidity of barrier islands allows their proper functioning as protectors of the mainland. The determination of land area versus water (or marsh) is a highly technical and continually improving science, with the National Geodetic Survey providing the standard. The difficulty in determining the land/water (or marsh) demarcation is due to the interaction of sea level changes, tides, land erosion, and other coastal land and water changes. According to the Georgia Department of Natural Resources, the demarcation of land versus water (or marsh) in the Georgia coastal area is valid for not longer than one year when private development is at issue. From a land area perspective, the Jekyll Island of 1996 is most likely not the Jekyll Island of 2009. In the past thirteen years, the above-mentioned influences have caused changes in the island's size. What is most important about this is that to be most responsible in adhering to the Egan law, the land area of Jekyll Island should be accurately determined before any further development occurs on Jekyll. The application of land calculations from 1996 that were based on a 1980 Department of Transportation aerial photo of Jekyll Island are likely to be inaccurate.

In December 2008, a Ph.D. student at the University of Georgia reported a revised land area for Jekyll Island, based on LIDAR technology. LIDAR bounces a laser beam from an airplane or satellite to thousands of ground-level points to determine elevation and contour. The use of LIDAR provides one of the most accurate measures of elevation available. The student's report was preliminary and awaiting verification from faculty. After being reviewed by faculty, the University tentatively reported that instead of 108 acres of land available for development on Jekyll, the more accurate figure was likely fifty-five acres. In response, Jekyll Island Authority spokesman Eric Garvey said: "We are comfortable that we are still well under the threshold" (Shelton 2008). After news of this student's work became public, the Jekyll Island Authority announced that it had done its own recalculation of island acreage using LIDAR. The recalculation was done by a private engineering firm, Thomas and Hutton of Brunswick, Georgia. I found it interesting that the money-strapped Jekyll Island Authority spent over $6,000 on a private contract, when they could have inquired about the student's research and worked with the University of Georgia's prestigious Center for Remote Sensing and Mapping Science. Instead, they dismissed the student's research and spent reportedly scarce funds on a private contract that duplicated the work.

After Thomas and Hutton had completed their study, the Jekyll Island Authority announced that 55.57 acres (not 108) were available for development. Thomas and Hutton's estimate, while mirroring the student's, was also a result of additional land development that had occurred on Jekyll since 1996. If the student had not taken this project on, and if the Jekyll Island Authority had not become aware of his work, would the Authority have proceeded on the assumption that they could develop 108 acres of the public's land, and thereby unwittingly violate the Mike Egan law?

Thomas and Hutton's estimate was based on the 1996 Master Plan definitions for developed and undeveloped land on Jekyll. I submitted an open records request to the Authority in March 2009, and was given a list of the developed acreage added by Thomas and Hutton's calculations. This included acreage at the boat ramp, bike path, parts of Pine Lakes Golf Course, land near the 4-H Center, and land around the churches. In the 1996 Master Plan, the Jekyll Island Authority considered the 65.36 acres of man-made water hazards located within the golf courses to be undeveloped land (p. 8). This was done despite the fact that the Master Plan also stated that "Cleared golf course areas" and "Lakes or ponds used for active recreation" were to be classified as developed (p. 6). In spite of the contradiction between pages 6 and 8 in the plan, the definition on page 6 is in line with the MacConnell Land Use Classification Scheme, used by the state of Massachusetts to classify land uses. The 65.36 acres of golf course hazards were not included in the list I received from the open records request, and therefore must still be incorrectly classified as undeveloped land by the Jekyll Island Authority. Jeff Watkins, President of the Georgia Planning Association, recently analyzed land use on Jekyll

These man-made golf course water hazards are classified as undeveloped land by the Jekyll Island Authority.

Island according to best practices in the planning profession. He concluded that 35.21 percent of Jekyll Island is developed, leaving 64.76 percent undeveloped. In his assessment, therefore, Jekyll Island is *already* over the thirty-five percent development cap.

The need for a periodic independent and professional update of land area demarcation, and especially a professional enumeration of developed versus undeveloped acres of Jekyll Island, is clear. Before any further development is begun, the need is critical. Dr. Thomas Jordan, co-director of the University of Georgia's Center for Remote Sensing and Mapping Science, said "Even preliminary results point to the fact that these questions need to be answered and that we need to do it properly" (Shelton 2008).

The Incorporation of Not Just Any Private Partner

In March 2007, the Jekyll Island Authority hired the Bleakly Advisory Group to identify the opportunities for incorporating a private partner to assist in the development of Jekyll Island. Recall that no scientific studies of visitors had been presented, and therefore presumably had not been done, to establish the need for development, or what kind of development the citizens of Georgia would deem most appropriate for their state park. The Bleakly Advisory Group's work was to include the drafting of a Request for Proposals (RFP) from private developers and assistance with the selection of a private partner. In 2008, the Bleakly Advisory Group was twice again hired, without competition, by the Jekyll Island Authority. The Bleakly Advisory Group's tasks in 2008 were to assess the economic feasibility of island development and the impacts of development on island population, housing, and lodging density. At the request of the Initiative to Protect Jekyll Island and Senator Jeff Chapman, the Bleakly Advisory Group's studies have been evaluated by nationally-recognized outdoor recreation scientists and natural resource economists. These experts have judged these studies as inappropriate for state park planning, and indeed, one of the studies includes highly misleading data and seriously flawed conclusions (See chapter 10).

The Authority's decision to bring a private development partner on board appears to have been made without public input and without any assessment of visitor needs and desires, or the potential public costs and benefits of increased development on Jekyll Island. In Chapter 3, you were introduced to the planning acronym VEE-SIPPI: Visitor Experiences, Environment, Science, Involvement, Park Purpose, and Interdisciplinary. As you read the following chapters, consider whether the Jekyll Island Authority has followed VEE-SIPPI, the guidelines that describe best practices for outdoor recreation planning.

In 2006 and early 2007, the Authority's vision of Jekyll Island's "revitalization" included large single family "estate" homes, a hotel, and condominiums on the environmentally-sensitive south end of Jekyll Island. Public opposition to this

Option 1

Beach

"The site is that is currently occupied by the 4-H Center and the soccer fields offers a substantial opportunity to increase the residential base of Jekyll Island...The proposed development would consist largely of single family homes, and a small number of condominiums. The single family lots would be on the scale of cottage homes and potentially larger estate homes."

Option 2

Beach

"This option alters the predominantly residential nature of the previous design and proposes a 350 key hotel, 30 villas, and 8 single family home sites. Similar to the previous scheme, this site would offer relative seclusion and direct beach access."

Option 3   Beach

"The third option returns to a predominantly residential design. It would consist of a 200 key hotel, 12 estate lots, and 4 single family home lots."

Southend Village was proposed for the area currently occupied by the 4-H Center and soccer fields. This proposal was part of a larger plan for Jekyll Island, developed by Cooper Carry for the Jekyll Island Authority (2006?, 17-18).

vision was widespread and unquestionable.

During the 2007 legislative session, state Representative Terry Barnard, R-Glennville, introduced House Bill 214. In its original form, House Bill 214 would have extended the lease from the state to the Jekyll Island Authority, in essence extending the existence of the Authority. This legislation was mentioned by Ben Porter in a letter to Governor Perdue dated February 6, 2007, as Porter accepted his appointment to the Jekyll Island Authority board.

Senator Jeff Chapman, R-Brunswick, responding to citizen alarm over the potential development of Jekyll's south end, introduced amendments to the bill which would prohibit further development on the south end and place a development cap on the total number of new private residences that could be constructed on Jekyll. Senator Chapman's amendments would also close a loophole that allowed parts of Jekyll Island to be sold. Negotiations on this bill came down to a nail-biting showdown between Senator Chapman and some of his fellow Republicans.

The *Atlanta Journal-Constitution* reported on this tense, late-night session:

> Chapman was an army of one against the five other conferees appointed by House and Senate leaders who prefer more, not less, development on Jekyll. "I'm willing to give in on the south end, but if you insist on (limiting) the number of residents, we don't have a deal," [Representative Terry] Barnard [(R-Glennville)] inveighed during the 6[:00] p.m. conference committee gathering. "We have compromised to the limit." Seventy-five minutes later, they were back in air-less Room 122. Frank Mirasola, a Jekyll resident, was shocked to see [Linger Longer lobbyist Joe] Tanner and [lobbyist Arthur "Skin"] Edge seated across from Chapman and Senator Ross Tolleson (R-Perry), attempting to hash out a compromise. "I didn't believe what I was seeing," Mirasola said. "Joe Tanner was running the meeting and the legislators were just sitting there.

That was surreal." (D. Chapman 2007)

If the name "Joe Tanner" sounds familiar to you, it should. Tanner was the former Commissioner of the Georgia Department of Natural Resources. Tanner was now a lobbyist at the Gold Dome, and his primary client was Linger Longer Communities. Of note is that the debate over House Bill 214 was held *before* the process that resulted in Linger Longer Communities being announced as the Jekyll Island Authority's private partner. How did it happen that Linger Longer Communities' lobbyist took part in the negotiations for House Bill 214 *before* the Jekyll Island Authority announced it was seeking a private partner? How was it that one of the sticking points of the bill was a limit on new private residences, such as condominiums and timeshares, to be built on Jekyll Island?

Following the late night compromise between Senator Chapman and the Republican leaders, the Georgia Legislature passed House Bill 214. After a long delay and considerable public pressure, Governor Sonny Perdue signed H.B. 214 into law on the last allowable day. Along with extending the Jekyll Island Authority lease, the bill restricted further development on the south end of Jekyll Island and prohibited the sale of Jekyll Island land. It also created a bicameral Legislative Oversight Committee to monitor the "revitalization" of Jekyll Island.

On July 15, 2007, Brandon Larrabee of the *Georgia Times Union* reported on the results of a Georgia Open

Records Act request. The paper reviewed hundreds of documents, and from that review concluded that

Contrary to his publicly maintained distance on the debate over Jekyll Island's future, the documents show Perdue's office was sometimes intimately involved in the debate over extending the Jekyll Island Authority's lease in hopes of luring private developers.

The documents also reveal ties between the governor's office and lobbyists for developers interested in Jekyll's potential for profit. Some of those developers are expected to be major players in the island's redevelopment, though Perdue insists he has no favorites.

House Bill 214, which Perdue signed in May, protects the island's ecologically fragile south end and bars the state from selling any Jekyll land. The original bill had none of those safeguards that were proposed by legislators outside Perdue's camp.

Recall that House Bill 214 created a Legislative Oversight Committee to monitor the "revitalization" of Jekyll Island. The Legislative Oversight Committee, however, has appeared to have only supported actions taken by the Jekyll Island Authority. I attended one of their meetings in Atlanta in 2008. The room was packed with citizens opposing the Jekyll Island Authority's "revitalization" plans. Nevertheless, the Oversight Committee praised the Jekyll Island Authority and barely acknowledged members of the public who were in attendance. Although it is appropriate for the Oversight Committee to support some Authority actions, it is perhaps more appropriate to question them, since by definition "oversight" means regulatory supervision. When widespread public opposition to Authority decisions is expressed, moreover, the Legislative Oversight Committee should be even more diligent in its supervision. (See Chapter 14 for a list of the members of the Legislative Oversight Committee.)

Among others, Representative Terry Barnard, R-Glennville, is a member of the Legislative Oversight Committee. Barnard, you may recall, refused to allow an upper limit on the number of new private residences to be built on Jekyll Island during negotiations for House Bill 214. Barnard is owner of Marsh Coast Investment Real Estate, Incorporated (http://marshcoast.com/), and sells properties at Shellman Bluff at Cooper's Point (http://marshcoast.com/custom5. shtml). One of the developers of Shellman Bluff is Ben Porter, currently a Jekyll Island Authority board member and former Chairman of the Authority (http://www.theledliegroup. com/about-us/news-and-views/a-premier-golden-isles-community-joins-the-ledlie-group-client-list/). I find it interesting, and perhaps a little disturbing, that a Legislative Oversight Committee member has a business relationship with a member of the board over which he has oversight. And coincidently, Jekyll Island Authority board member

Ben Porter was a member of the Georgia Department of Natural Resources Advisory Board in the late 1990s, at the same time as Jamie Reynolds. Reynolds is one of the principals in Linger Longer Communities, the Jekyll Island Authority's private partner in state park development. During that same period in the late 1990s, Joe Tanner, now a Linger Longer lobbyist, was the Commissioner of the Department of Natural Resources. Senator Eric Johnson, an ex-officio member of the Jekyll Island Authority board, is running for the office of Governor of Georgia in 2010. His campaign finance chairman is Linger Longer's Jamie Reynolds (http://www.connectsavannah.com/news/article/100578/).

In April 2007, the Jekyll Island Authority held only one meeting for public input into the Request for Proposal (RFP) process for the selection of a private partner. This meeting was not widely publicized, was held on Jekyll Island, and was attended primarily by island residents. After the Jekyll Island Authority's consultant, Ken Bleakly of the Bleakly Advisory Group, outlined the RFP and before the public input session started, all but one of the Authority board members departed. They missed hearing the comments of Jekyll's residents who attended the meeting. They missed the Initiative to Protect Jekyll Island's presentation of over 100 pages of testimony from Jekyll visitors from around the state calling for minimal, if any, development beyond the rebuilding of Jekyll's aging oceanfront hotels. What happened to the Master Plan's objective 5? That was the one emphasizing the Authority's intent to listen to widespread public input.

On June 1, 2007, the Jekyll Island Authority issued the RFP to select a private development partner. The scope of development outlined in the RFP included a forty-five acre town center. The RFP invited developers to present concepts for this town center. The Jekyll Island Authority received four proposals, including one from Linger Longer Communities. On September 24, 2007, the Jekyll Island Authority announced the selection of Linger Longer Communities as its private partner.

The Jekyll Island Authority and Linger Longer Communities

Was the selection of Linger Longer Communities as the Jekyll Island Authority's private partner inevitable? Recall Linger Longer lobbyist Joe Tanner's April 2007 involvement in opposing legislation that could have limited the number of new condominiums and timeshares built on Jekyll Island. Prior to the selection of Linger Longer Communities, there were rumors of their certain selection. Wilson Smith, an area attorney and former talk radio personality, tells a part of the story below. The following is printed from a "What Is Goin' On?" podcast by Smith, published on October 12, 2007. In this podcast, Smith interviews Wade Shealy of the Jekyll Island Revitalization Group. Shealy's company was one of the competitors in the private partner contest.

If this interview with Wade Shealy of the Jekyll

Island Company doesn't piss you off, nothing will. On September 24, 2007, the Jekyll Island Authority.... awarded a redevelopment project, worth [m]illions, to Mercer Reynolds' company, Linger Longer. You know Reynolds as in Reynolds Plantation on Lake Oconee....

In June 2007, the Jekyll Island Authority solicited proposals (via a Request For Proposals, or RFP) to develop forty-five acres (the acreage specified in the RFP) on Jekyll Island. Bids were turned in by the middle of August. Four companies submitted proposals: The Jekyll Island Revitalization Group, Linger Longer Communities, Cousins Coastal Ventures, and Trammell Crow Company.

One company's proposal, Cousins, was culled because only the top three could be considered for the award. The winner was announced on September 24th by Ken Bleakly, the consultant hired by the Jekyll Island Authority to oversee the process.

The selection committee was composed of two employees of the Jekyll Island Authority, together with the Chairman, Benjamin (Ben) G. Porter of Macon and Jekyll Island Authority Board Member, Robert W. (Bob) Krueger of Hawkinsville, GA, both of whom were appointed to the Jekyll Island Authority by Perdue in August 2006.

When [Bleakly] announced Linger Longer as the winner, he said the reason was their proposal provided more green space. He seems to have forgotten to mention that the reason their plan had more green space was that it included a nineteen acre park that was not located on the forty-five acres specified in the RFP.

QUESTIONS OF THE DAY: (1) Why is it that the other three companies were never told they could include an additional nineteen acres if they wanted to? (2) If this were an innocent mistake, why weren't the other companies allowed to resubmit their proposals based on an amended RFP? (3) Why wasn't Linger Longer's bid thrown out (rather than Cousins') for failing to comply with the specifications of the RFP?) (4) Why didn't Ken Bleakly get in trouble for screwing up the process?

Being awarded the Master Developer contract means profits in the millions of dollars, maybe even hundreds of millions. While that may be a hell of a lot of money, the risk of failure, poor sales, etc. is always there. But if this project is to be so lucrative, if Jekyll is to be the "Jewel of Georgia," it is a disgrace to have the award of the contract sullied by these types of shenanigans. And that is putting it lightly!

You should also know that Senator Eric Johnson and Representative Jerry Keen are advisory members of the Jekyll Island Authority Board. I haven't heard about any outrage from them. Wonder what their advice was?

During the selection process, each bidder had an opportunity to respond to questions from the Jekyll Island Authority board. In August 2007, after the Authority queried Linger Longer, they responded that they "could not recommend the financial return [suggested by Linger Longer's proposal] to [the] Jekyll Island Authority's Board as sound financial stewardship for the future of Jekyll Island." The Authority continued by asking Linger Longer to explain how they would "substantially improve the financial return to Jekyll Island Authority from your proposal over the initial fifteen years…"

Linger Longer responded by making financial concessions which apparently made their proposal the most attractive of the three, along with their additional acres of greenspace. In a later chapter, we will see what happened to these concessions in the signed contract between the Authority and Linger Longer Communities.

That was 2007. The unusual RFP process that resulted in Linger Longer Communities becoming the Jekyll Island Authority's private partner has largely been forgotten. Also forgotten is that the Jekyll Island Authority has never properly established the need for further development of Jekyll Island.

On April 1, 2008, Wilson Smith posed the question: "Is the proposed development necessary?" In response to his own question, Smith said:

The answer depends on your choice of goals. [Jim] Langford of Linger Longer contends it will generate $100 million in income for the Jekyll Island Authority over ten or more years. It is hard to argue against such a project if your goal is to make as much money as possible. Not only that, but this project is just the first that the Jekyll Island Authority is contemplating. Presumably, the Jekyll Island Authority wants even more income. The question is why? The answer to that question is not written in some brochure or noted on the Jekyll Island Authority Website. The motives of the Jekyll Island Authority can only be judged in the context of its actions and conduct regarding the development and promotion of the project.

Linger Longer Communities' First Town Center Proposal

Public outcry against Linger Longer Communities' first town center proposal, the one advanced in response to the RFP, was widespread from across the state. The Initiative to Protect Jekyll Island (IPJI), a grassroots citizen group, reported heavy opposition to Linger Longer Communities' plans for the island. IPJI Co-Director Mindy Egan, in a letter to Linger Longer's Jim Langford, asked that public input solicited by Linger Longer Communities to their town center proposal be made public. Langford's written response to Egan, dated July 14, 2007 and accessed by me from the Initiative to Protect

Jekyll Island Web site, was to outline the many ways Linger Longer Communities had solicited and received feedback from the public. In summary, however, Langford told Egan, "But most of the feedback is too general and too brief to be of much real value beyond expressions of sentiment both for and against the project. Organizing or compiling a summary of this feedback would be very difficult and costly — far exceeding any value gained." Linger Longer went to a lot of trouble to collect public input, but told Egan that it was too much trouble to analyze it. Langford's statement to Egan seemed to imply that there would have been little value in summarizing what the public had to say.

In 2007, I attended one of the public input meetings coordinated by Linger Longer Communities. At this meeting in Atlanta, held right before the afternoon's rush hour on the Tuesday before Thanksgiving, Jim Langford made a presentation about Linger Longer Communities' town center proposal. His presentation was videotaped. Following his presentation, the public was allowed to ask questions, and although the camera was trained on Langford, public questions and comments appeared to be audio-taped. Most of the public comments made during that meeting were critical of the town center proposal. There was one special and impassioned plea from a ten year-old girl not to develop Jekyll Island. I found Langford's presentation on YouTube, in a series of five videos entitled "Rediscover Jekyll Island Public Input Sessions." The videos, although they were labeled "Public Input Sessions," only included Langford's presentation. Dozens of comments were offered by Georgians to Linger Longer during these public input sessions. These citizens took the time to attend what they thought was to be a legitimate listening session on the town center proposal. These comments, including those from that articulate ten year-old girl, were never made public, and were a part of the collection of comments that, according to Langford, would have been too costly to summarize.

The Jekyll Island Authority invited visitor comments on the town center proposal at its offices at Villa Ospo on Jekyll Island between November 2007 and March 2008 (not exactly the busiest time on Jekyll). The Authority received 272 written comments on the Linger Longer Communities proposed town center. It did not, however, summarize the public's comments. The Jekyll Island Authority told me it had forwarded a copy of these written public comments to Linger Longer Communities, and there was no indication of what Linger Longer Communities did with these comments, if they did anything at all. I decided to analyze the comments myself, and acquired copies of them via a Georgia Open Records Act request. I found that 72.4 percent of the public comments expressed opposition to Linger Longer Communities' town center proposal. Twenty-two percent were either neutral or I was unable to ascertain support or opposition. An example of this kind of comment was "Please keep the beachfront open" and "Please protect Jekyll's natural treasures." Only 5.5 percent of the comments received by the Jekyll Island Authority at Villa Opso expressed support for Linger Longer Communities' town center proposal.

The Initiative to Protect Jekyll Island's Web site includes each one of the thousands of public comments the organization received regarding Linger Longer Communities' town center proposal. I downloaded them in the spring of 2009, and they filled 214 pages. Some are presented in this book in italics at the beginning of each chapter. Here are a few additional representative examples:

V.M.B., Ashburn, GA — If beach goers want to stay in crowded back to back condos and hotels with strip malls on every corner — let them go to Panama City. Jekyll deserves to remain the jewel that she is. Untouched as much as possible to offer a true vision of the beach experience. What would Rockefeller and Vanderbilt say about the proposals?

A.H., Atlanta, GA — My biggest concern, despite the obvious harm to the local ecosystem, is the subversive way this proposal has been implemented. It lends one to think that the development proposed by Linger Longer is harmful. Who will pay for this? Who will pay for it if tourism does not improve the local economy? The Georgia taxpayer, who will not be able to afford the proposed Jekyll Island accommodations, will have the pay for it.

K.W., Winder, GA — There are too few areas left that have

not been "sold out" to the big developers. They are ruining our state — to benefit a few and restrict access for the general public. Jekyll is one of the few public areas that still has the option of remaining a limited development resource. It would be a real shame to see it over-developed.

Public opposition to the town center proposal was mostly focused on the redevelopment of the parking area to the north of the Convention Center. Citizens did not want to lose beach access or the ocean view made available by the parking, picnicking, and beach access area. In response, State Senator Jeff Chapman (R), whose district includes Jekyll Island, and Representative Debbie Buckner

The beach just north of the current convention center's location, with its wide beach accessible at all tide levels, is favored by Jekyll's visitors.

(D-Columbus) introduced legislation in 2008 to protect this beach area. Legislative leaders prevented this legislation from reaching the floor for a full vote. For a list of Georgia legislators blocking the legislation that would have legally protected this favored recreation area, see Appendix 4.

In early 2008, it became clear that the beach area in question would be under the jurisdiction of Georgia's Shore Protection Act (O.G.C.A. 2-5-230, et seq.). Under the provisions of this Act, Linger Longer Communities and the Jekyll Island Authority would have to seek permits from the Georgia Department of Natural Resources for development within the Shore Protection Zone. Had they pursued the project without the proper permits, the Jekyll Island Authority may have faced legal action, and the pursuit of permits might delay the project.

According to former Authority board member Ed Boshears, Jim Langford (now retired) of Linger Longer was told four months prior (in December 2007) by the Department of Natural Resources that the Authority would need a permit to build within the Shore Protection Zone. For weeks, the Authority continued to entertain plans to build within that area but did not seek a permit. Boshears believes that Authority member Ben Porter and Langford hoped that legislative leaders might exempt the development from needing a permit. This did not happen. On April 2, 2008, the Jekyll Island Authority announced that the area in question would instead be developed as a public park. This park would include a Discovery Center, a playground, and a miniature golf course. Linger Longer Communities would go back to the drawing board, ostensibly because of public opposition to their first town center proposal.

The new public park will be completely funded as part of $50 million in State General Obligation Bonds, which, reportedly, are to be paid back by the Jekyll Island Authority through increased visitor revenue. The increased revenue is expected to come from redevelopment and further development of the island, as well as an increase in entrance fees. The General Obligation Bonds were approved by the Georgia General Assembly in their 2009 session, in the midst of a budget crisis. Approximately five months after the bonds were approved, Georgia Governor Sonny Perdue mandated the furlough of all public teachers for three days to save $33 million in state funds. Announcing these furloughs, the Governor said, "I know it hurts. A lot of people are hurt in this economy" (Jones 2009b).

The beach area protected under the Shore Protection Act, however, may still not be safe from the bulldozer. In 2009, the protection offered by the Shore Protection Act came under attack by the state Senate leadership. Senators Ross Tolleson, Eric Johnson, and Tommie Williams introduced Senate Bill 229, legislation that would have shut out public opposition to any decision made by the Department of Natural Resources. This bill, in effect, would shield administration decisions from proper judicial oversight, including any decisions made regarding the Shore Protection

Zone on Jekyll Island. These three senators have all indicated their support for the Jekyll Island development project. A bit further on, you will find that Senator Tommie Williams said he doesn't know or care how much money Linger Longer will make on the Jekyll Island deal. And worth noting, both he and Senator Tolleson are members of the Jekyll Island Legislative Oversight Committee.

A Change in the Jekyll Island Authority's Leadership

Amidst the turbulence of early 2008, the Jekyll Island Authority hired a new executive director. C. Jones Hooks, a Metter, Georgia native and most recently the President and CEO of the Hampton Roads Economic Development Alliance in southeastern Virginia, joined the Jekyll Island Authority in time to shepherd the revitalization contract to completion. Of note, the Jekyll Island Authority board did not hire someone with professional outdoor recreation, state park, environmental, or even public service experience, but instead selected a professional in economic development.

Mr. Hooks has been cultivating relationships with the business community of Brunswick and garnering support for the development of Jekyll. Although Mr. Hooks is being asked to integrate Jekyll as a participant in Georgia's greater coastal community, that community apparently does not involve groups like the Center for a Sustainable Coast, the Glynn County Environmental Coalition, or the Altamaha Riverkeepers. Being the executive director of the Jekyll

Island Authority does not appear to require coordination with the Department of Community Affairs Coastal Comprehensive Plan or with the Georgia Statewide Comprehensive Outdoor Recreation Plan. Judging from the status of the conservation plan and the lack of environmental assessments, the Jekyll Island Authority board does not appear to be placing the priority for Mr. Hooks' time on protecting and enhancing the natural environment of Jekyll. Neither does the executive director appear to be urged by the Jekyll Island Authority board to sustain the visitor experiences loved by so many Georgians. Surely, if they were, Mr. Hooks would be following a different course of action.

Chapter 7
Private Development Is "Necessary"

S.L., Ashburn, GA — Jekyll Island has been our vacation choice since our children were three and six. They are now thirty-seven and forty and there are now four grandchildren between six years and ten months. The tradition has been continued with them. We recently spent a week in a five-bedroom, three-bath rental, all ten of us. It was a very special week, as have all of them been over the years. In the early years, the affordability was very important, and still is. We also attended Beach Music for about twelve years. The history, the ecosystem, the specialness of the island must be preserved. My children and I have had our chance to love the island and it is my hope that my grandchildren will be given the same opportunity.

The public appears to be at the back of the Jekyll Island Authority bus, if they are on it at all. The Authority likes to note that Jekyll Island is not in the state park system, operates under a self-sustaining mandate, and is managed by an Authority. The Georgia Code, however, states that "'Park' means present and future parks, parkways, park and recreational resources and facilities of the state or any department, agency, or institution of the state, and any such facility constituting part of the State Parks System and *shall specifically include Jekyll Island State Park.*" (O.C.G.A. § 12-3-231, Sec. 5) (2007; emphasis mine)

The claim of being outside of the state park system, moreover, is no reason to discard the accepted practices of public outdoor recreation and land use planning. Even when Georgia code requires a procedure of the Jekyll Island Authority, questions have been raised about whether those proper procedures have been followed.

I am referring to Public Law 12-3-235, which gives the Jekyll Island Authority the power:

(6) To plan, survey, subdivide, improve, administer, construct, erect, acquire, own, repair, remodel, maintain, add to, extend, improve, equip, operate, and manage projects as defined in Code Section 12-3-231 (see below), to be located on property owned or leased by the authority, the cost of any such project to be paid from its income, from the proceeds of revenue anticipation certificates of the authority, or from such proceeds and any grant from the United States or any agency or instrumentality thereof, or from the State of Georgia; **provided, however, that the authority shall not undertake any such activity having a projected cost of over $1 million unless it has first evaluated the feasibility of involving private**

persons or entities in the development, construction, operation, and management of the authority's existing projects and such proposed activities and has filed a copy of such evaluation with the Office of Planning and Budget and with the Recreational Authorities Overview Committee; (emphasis mine)

I submitted a Georgia Open Records Act request to the Office of Planning and Budget (OPB) and the Recreational Authorities Overview Committee for a copy of the required feasibility study. The OPB replied that there was no such document on file. The Recreation Authorities Overview Committee, seeming to disregard the Georgia Open Records Act, never responded. When I asked the Jekyll Island Authority, through a Georgia Open Records Act request, if it had performed such an evaluation, the reply via email on July 9, 2008 was that such evaluation applied only to revenue-bonded projects: "Because the 2007 RFP was not a project to be paid for with the proceeds of revenue bonds of the authority, the feasibility evaluation was neither required by law, nor performed." I am not sure if the Jekyll Island Authority was legally right or wrong, but it certainly did not adhere to the spirit of the law, which appears to me to call for a feasibility study for projects over $1 million that include a private partner. The law must certainly have been intended to cover the project itself, not the request for proposals.

Senator Jeff Chapman also filed a Georgia Open Records Act request to determine if the Jekyll Island Authority had performed the required feasibility study. He was answered by Assistant Attorney General George Zier. You may remember Mr. Zier as the individual holding (up) the draft Jekyll Island conservation plan. Counselor Zier informed Senator Chapman that the feasibility requirement had been satisfied in the form of the RFP itself. This makes no sense, not to mention that it contradicts the information I was given in response to my own Georgia Open Records Act request for the same information. And if the RFP was intended to satisfy the law's requirement, why were no copies filed with the appropriate governmental units?

A guest editorial in the Athens, Georgia weekly newspaper *Flagpole* examined this omission of the Jekyll Island Authority. In noting that the requirement to conduct a feasibility study is "a substantive requirement meant to produce a document, copies of which must be filed with two other agencies," concerned citizen Leon Galis (2009) observed:

> What's the point of such a requirement? The General Assembly, while preferring private investment over public funding, also recognized that Jekyll Island's public purpose presents challenges for private enterprises that not every developer will be willing or able to meet. Accordingly, the law requires that the Authority fully apprise potential private partners of those challenges and evaluate the feasibility of engaging them based on their willingness and ability to serve Jekyll Island's public mission. That's a

reasonable approach to securing the public interest in a cost-effective way.

However, two Authority representatives have admitted in writing that the feasibility study was never done. Both admissions were accompanied by different equally tortured explanations for why the Authority wasn't obligated to conduct the study, notwithstanding the plain language of the statute. So much for complying "with all law."

The Jekyll Island Authority Complains

In a March 28, 2008 letter to the General Assembly, former Jekyll Island Authority chairman and current board member Ben Porter alleged that the only opposition to the proposed development of Jekyll Island was coming from "a small select group of individuals, most of whom live on Jekyll Island," while "the vast majority of Georgians want to see responsible development of Jekyll Island and do not share the views of the minority who want to close the gate behind them so they may enjoy their own utopia." Porter warned the General Assembly not to allow a "small group of residents and some in the environmental lobby to affect policy to the detriment of hundreds of thousands of Georgians who want to see Jekyll Island returned to its heyday." Yet the Initiative to Protect Jekyll Island represents some 7,000 members statewide, not just Jekyll Island residents, and 3,000 more members from states across America. IPJI, as it is called, has never opposed responsible development. In a February 2008 opinion editorial to the *Atlanta Journal Constitution*, written one month before Porter's accusations, IPJI co-director David Egan said:

> Everyone agrees that Jekyll Island State Park is in need of revitalization. Its oceanfront hotels have deteriorated, public dissatisfaction with its lodgings has grown, and visits have fallen off....The truth is that Jekyll's visitors stand for responsible revitalization. They support hotel and convention center redevelopment, the enhancement of the island's amenities and recreational opportunities, the further development of Jekyll's nature tourism potential, and a ban on new development near Jekyll's environmentally sensitive areas, particularly the beachfront of this delicate barrier island.

It appears that Porter was trying the old trick of marginalizing the opposition by calling it a small, self-serving minority. The reality is that a growing number of Georgians have been vocal in their opposition to this give-away of their state park. This is evident in the growing membership of IPJI and the hundreds of blog postings from people statewide in opposition to the increased development of Jekyll Island State Park. An opinion editorial written by me in the *Atlanta Journal-Constitution* in October 2009 resulted in a large number of responses decrying the Jekyll development deal, with letters to the editor printed almost daily through mid-November. Of all the letters printed, only one supported the Linger Longer development, and that letter was written by Jekyll Island Authority marketing director Eric Garvey. The public, it appears, is not in support of the new development being planned for their island state park.

The Bleakly Advisory Group Strikes Again

On September 15, 2008, the Jekyll Island Authority revealed a preliminary analysis performed by the Bleakly Advisory Group. The Bleakly Group had again been selected without competition. There may be some wisdom in contracting with the same consultant time after time, but if it is the public's business, it seems to me that other consultants should at least have an opportunity to compete for the contract. This time, the Bleakly Advisory Group analyzed the long-term financial needs of Jekyll Island, and the degree of development needed to provide the Authority with the revenue to service those needs.

Dr. Ken Cordell, a public land economist with a specialty in outdoor recreation, reviewed the Bleakly Advisory Group's financial analysis and made this important observation in an email to me dated November 28, 2009:

> The [Bleakly Advisory Group] proposal for doing the development impact analysis stated as the key question, "What is a sustainable level of future development that both protects the island's

environmental resources and delivers the type of visitor experience that is expected of Georgia's Jewel?" But that is the wrong question. The correct question is: "How can Jekyll Island utilize its unique situation and rich natural and cultural resources to insure long-term sustainable management of the island as a state park, enhance visitor experiences, and protect Jekyll's unique natural and cultural character?" The emphasis should be on visitors and park protection, not on development.

The distinction is important. The Bleakly Advisory Group began with the assumption that future development is the inevitable key to Jekyll's future. As pointed out by Cordell, this seems to put the cart before the horse. Cordell's question begins with the assumption that Jekyll Island's situation and resources should be leveraged to insure financial security, enhance visitor experiences, and protect the environment. It does not assume *a priori* that more development is necessary. By making the assumption up front that more development is necessary, Bleakly most likely biased his own analysis, whether intentional or not.

Cordell has also been troubled by the lack of citizen participation. The IPJI, representing over 10,000 members, asked to have input into the Bleakly Advisory Group's proposal process, but its request was discounted by the Jekyll Island Authority. In addition, neither the Jekyll Island Authority nor the Bleakly Advisory Group has done any state-wide, random, scientifically appropriate surveys to determine what Jekyll's visitors want from their visitation experiences and how they envision Jekyll's future. It is well known that state parks have a unique character, similar to their big sister national parks. However, the particular visitor experiences, expectations, and values related to Jekyll Island have yet to be defined. The best data we have of visitor experiences on Jekyll Island come from the nearly 10,000 comments received by IPJI through their Web site. A small sample of these comments is given throughout this book in italics. A compilation of the comments are available on the IPJI's Web site at www.savejekyllisland.org/pubOP.html.

Cordell emphasized the lack of public involvement allowed by the Jekyll Island Authority and the firm's proposal. He noted that the 2004 Master Plan Update called for a public participation process:

> There appears still to be significant opportunity for full engagement of all publics in interpretation and evaluation of the Bleakly Advisory Group study, in development of scenario selections (across a full range of options), in selecting impact indicators and measurement approaches (biophysical and social), in forecasting Jekyll Island's future, and in reviewing proposals associated with different future scenarios. This can include identifying and defining criteria for social, economic, and environmental sustainability, as well as for sustainability of quality visitor experiences. (2008, 5)

What is even more intriguing about Cordell's assessment is that he shared his concerns in a person-to-person meeting with Authority Executive Director Jones Hooks and staff members Jim Broadwell and John Hunter on September 19, 2008. Cordell said in an email to me dated November 23, 2009,

> As you can see, the meeting with Hooks was on the 19th of Aug. 2008. The briefing paper I presented to them is attached. I did say that the Bleakly approach was inappropriate for planning a state park. I also told them that there are well established public park planning techniques. I also critiqued their visitation stats at which point John Hunter said something like, "Oh, those were never meant to be the official visitation trend numbers."

The following comes directly from Cordell's briefing paper, a copy of which he gave to Hooks.

Platform for discussion:

- **Modern public land planning is an open, participatory, and collaborative process** that is built upon a comprehensive and broad-scale evaluation of relevant social, economic, and ecological conditions and trends. From this open process comes a clear statement of mission, vision, and goals of management.

- Because it concerns a publicly owned resource, federal, state, or local government **public land planning requires more steps and added considerations,** when compared with private sector business planning.

- Jekyll Island State Park is public land and for any public land, the process of developing **a shared vision of the future** seems to offer the best opportunity for actively engaging the public as a partner in planning.

- **Jekyll Island's planning should tier** to the Georgia Statewide Comprehensive Outdoor Recreation Plan and the to the shared vision for state parks and historic sites as spelled out in the Georgia State Parks and Historic Sites *New Day, New Way* Strategic Plan.

- The **shared vision for Georgia State Parks** is as follows: "to become a national model for quality service, resource protection, outdoor recreational opportunities, ecosystems management and interpretation of heritage."

- An **opportunity to advance the Georgia State Parks vision** is available now through modification of the approach to be/being used by JIA and the Bleakly Group to conduct a long-term development impact analysis. (emphasis in original)

It was as if Dr. Cordell, an internationally-known expert in outdoor recreation planning, had never had that meeting with Hooks. The Bleakly analysis was accepted, as it was submitted, by Hooks and the Jekyll Island Authority board. Further, the report never had the benefit of widespread public review. In his analysis, Cordell noted ways that the Bleakly Advisory Group and the Jekyll Island Authority might have gathered public input:

A principal means for engaging the public is through application of surveying. Surveying various publics and visitors is widely accepted and used as a means of making contact with citizens, visitors, or special interests. Most ordinary Georgians cannot attend meetings and most will not have notification of opportunities for public participation. Surveys take the issues to the citizen in their homes or during a visit and can be conducted by mail, phone, in-person, on-site and via the internet. An overview of a few recent surveys found concerning Jekyll Island can be helpful. Based on the composition of these data, it seems a statewide survey of Georgians and Jekyll Island visitors and other interests is needed. (2008, 5)

Based on the evidence so far, it does not appear that the opportunity for authentic public input has been adequately provided by the Jekyll Island Authority, Linger Longer Communities, or the Bleakly Advisory Group. Following that meeting between Cordell and Hooks in September 2008, moreover, it seems fair to say that the Jekyll Island Authority had heard, from a respected expert, that the kind of process and analysis being used for its planning was inappropriate for a state park, and was not in line with best practices in the outdoor recreation profession. Why, following this revelation, would it not have changed course? Instead, the Authority continued with its inappropriate business-oriented, revenue-maximizing approach to determine the future of Jekyll Island State Park.

In an email discussion with me in early January 2010, Jekyll Island Authority Executive Director Jones Hooks insisted that a business model is appropriate for Jekyll Island State Park, since the Authority must be self-sustaining in its operations. I disagree. *Every* park manager must be mindful of the bottom line, and operate within a budget. A business model is an inappropriate model for any public park. A state park's managing entity must identify *first* what the park's purpose is, and ask the public what kind of experiences they value. After understanding this, a state park's management should then determine how to deliver what the public wants, within its budget. Even commercial businesses ask the public for input, in the form of focus group sessions. For Jekyll Island State Park, public preferences might express the desire for *less* infrastructure and more nature, which would suggest fewer dollars needed for capital improvements and operations. This is at odds with the current management approach on

Jekyll, which claims an ever escalating need for capital improvements and, consequently, the need for more development to pay for those improvements.

A Representative Board?

On October 4, 2008, Wilson Smith conducted an interview on his radio show, this time with attorney and former Jekyll Island Authority Board Member Ed Boshears. Mr. Boshears had been the only board member openly questioning the development plans for Jekyll Island. Boshears, according to Smith, "takes seriously his responsibility as a trustee of state property set aside for enjoyment by the people of Georgia."

Boshears had been consequently removed from the Jekyll Island Authority board, by way of not being reappointed to another term by Governor Perdue. This was in spite of his request to remain on the board, and in spite of letters to Governor Perdue from citizens requesting that Boshears remain a board member. I know there were letters because I wrote one. It is true that Boshears' term was set to expire, yet other board members have been reappointed by the governor. For example, Governor Perdue reappointed board members Sybil Lynn, Steve Croy, and Ben Porter in 2009. Of course, these other board members were not asking the same hard questions as Boshears. In 2009, every member of the Jekyll Island Authority board appeared to support the private development project. In late 2009, the professional affiliations of Authority board members were primarily with banking, real estate, and business. The current board members appear to have little or no training, experience, or familiarity with professional outdoor recreation and public land planning and management. All, with the exception of Sybil Lynn, are white males. This is not an accurate mirror of the gender and racial diversity of Georgia. I wonder how Governor Perdue can believe this board represents our state's population, or how such a board is able to knowledgeably set appropriate policy for a public asset, such as a state park. (See Appendix 5 for more information about the professional backgrounds of the Jekyll Island Authority Board of Directors.)

The Jekyll Island Authority's Attempts to Justify the Need for Development

Between 2007 and 2009, the Jekyll Island Authority's stated justification for embarking on the private partner development project changed. One of the earliest justifications was that the hotels on Jekyll Island had become so run down that no one wanted to visit anymore. I wondered who let the hotels' conditions deteriorate. After reflecting on this, I concluded that the Jekyll Island Authority must be responsible, as the managing agency of the island. Through a Georgia Open Records Act Request on April 8, 2009, I asked for all of the inspection reports of hotels on Jekyll Island from 1996 to demolition or the present time. The reports, prepared by Bare Associates International, abruptly stopped in 2004, leading me to conclude that inspections were no longer being conducted. The Bare reports contained information about comprehensive and detailed hotel inspection services that included employee behavior and service, hotel condition, and food quality. Once these reports were not longer available, the Jekyll Island Authority had no uniform, periodic, systematic, and independent way to monitor the physical conditions and guest services of Jekyll Island's hotels. This also removed the opportunity to identify and correct substandard hotel conditions as they occurred. As the hotels deteriorated, the Jekyll Island Authority claimed the need to tear them down and start over. This need for redevelopment, subsequently, was also used as a reason to expand the plans to include even more hotels, timeshares, condominiums, and a new retail town center.

In spite of the Jekyll Island Authority's claim of declining hotel visitation, in 2006 Eric Garvey, the Jekyll Island Authority's marketing director, had a few interesting words about Jekyll's hotel occupancy. The *Brunswick News* reported: "Record revenues are predicted this year for several Jekyll Island hotels. 'The hotels that have committed management are doing great,' Garvey said.....'The story about the revenue drop off between the 2004 and 2005 fiscal years is weather'" (Starr 2006).

Compare Garvey's statement with other statements made by the Jekyll Island Authority. One of these is that visitation had dropped precipitously over the past two decades. (This argument was also made by now-Linger Longer lobbyist Joe Tanner in the late 1970s, eventually resulting in a change to the current board structure [Law number 823, 1984].) To provide support for this claim, in 2007 the Jekyll Island Authority produced information gleaned from their own traffic counts as recorded at the island's entry fee station. This information indicated a sudden fifty percent drop in vehicular traffic to Jekyll Island in 1997. This, they claimed, was just a part of the steady decline in visitation over the years. I submitted a Georgia Open Records Act request aimed at understanding how the Jekyll Island Authority produced its analysis of visitation. Its response claimed that the Authority calculated visitation estimates by hand and did not keep a copy of the procedure used to do the calculations, or even a copy of the calculations.

Beachgoers enjoy a day on Jekyll Island's beach in 2009.

In a second Georgia Open Records Act request, I asked to review whatever paperwork the Jekyll Island Authority could share regarding its determination of visitation decline. I was told that they could make copies of the papers they worked from, or I could come to Jekyll and go through the papers myself. Unfortunately for me, this meant I could wade through 180,000 pieces of paper at the Authority's offices for the bargain price of $425 (to pay for the guard), or I could pay them $46,500 to copy the 180,000 pieces of paper (Johnston 2008). Needless to say, the process the Jekyll Island Authority used to determine its visitation figures was never made public.

I find it both incredible and irresponsible that the Jekyll Island Authority could not reproduce the analytical process they used to make the claim of declining visitation, especially with so much at stake for Georgia's citizens.

An analysis by outdoor recreation expert Dr. Ken Cordell showed the sudden drop in visitation in 1997 to be a result of a change in the way the Authority counted vehicles entering the island. Prior to 1997, all cars entering the island were counted in the visitor traffic totals. Beginning in 1997, cars with annual passes were no longer counted, leading to an apparent and highly questionable drop of over one million visitors.

When this information was made public, the Authority switched to another data source. This time, they used Department of Transportation (DOT) traffic counts for the Jekyll causeway. These data seemed to offer support for the Authority's claim of a fifty percent drop in visitation over the past twenty years.

Dr. Ken Cordell, the public land economist and outdoor recreation expert cited earlier, conducted his own analysis of the DOT vehicular counts (See Chapter 10 for more detail). Cordell concluded that the use of DOT estimates for visitation was unreliable, primarily because of the DOT's sampling method. For example, the DOT's vehicular counts were taken at different times of the year, including the off-season. Cordell noted that vehicular counts should be taken in the same season every year, and preferably in every season. In some years, the DOT did not sample at all. DOT sampling also occurred over just a one or two-day span of time in the years sampling was done. Finally, Cordell speculated that the drop in traffic between 1996 and 1997 had to be caused by something other than an actual reduction in cars entering the island, as hotel occupancy during those years did not change significantly.

The Jekyll Island Authority has now produced what are reasonably accurate counts of the visitation drop. The Authority says that visitation has dropped twenty percent. This is no surprise, given that more than thirty percent of Jekyll's hotel rooms have been demolished in recent years as part of the Jekyll Island Authority's hotel redevelopment program.

In his lamentations, Jekyll Island Authority board member Ben Porter longed for a return to Jekyll's heyday. Prior to access by automobile, there were, understandably, few visitors to the island. In the 1950s, visitation was encouraged through the leasing of lots for homes. In the early 1960s, Jekyll Island was still a part of the segregated south. During this decade, segregation on Jekyll Island was successfully challenged by the local and state NAACP. Visitation was up and by the year 1965, Jekyll Island's budget was on solid footing (Martin and McCash 2003). By the late 1970s, DNR Commissioner Joe Tanner was complaining that visitation was falling off. His complaint, however, was registered in a decade of rampant inflation in the United States, with oil prices and interest rates high. In 1973 and 1979, moreover, oil supplies were tight nationwide. It is no surprise, therefore, that visits to Jekyll Island would have declined during this decade. In the 1980s, Summer Waves water park was constructed and the historic district began getting its facelift. If the number of hotel rooms rented is used as a marker, visitation to Jekyll began to rebound in the mid-1980s through 2001, when hotel room rentals were at their highest level. The third highest room rentals occurred in 2000. These figures run counter to the Jekyll Island Authority's claim that visitation has been declining for the past twenty years. Recall that in 2006, Eric Garvey proclaimed a record year for revenues on Jekyll Island. From what I can tell, Jekyll Island's visitation has seen some of the normal fluctuations one would expect from year to year, in response to changing general economic conditions (and in the first decade of the 21st century, three demolished hotels). Over time, however, it appears to me that visitation has been in line with what one would expect, and in fact has remained relatively healthy in these uncertain economic times.

Another justification for island development came from the reported dire financial condition of the Jekyll Island Authority. In 2007, one year after claiming record revenues for the island, the Jekyll Island Authority claimed to be operating in the red. I submitted a Georgia Open Records Act request for their publicly released annual reports, and discovered that the Authority operated in the black every year except one. In fact, according to the Georgia Department of Audits and Accounts, the Jekyll Island Authority, in its publicly-issued annual financial statements in 2006, under-reported its revenue by nearly $2 million. This occurred even while the full accounting of the Authority's books sent to Atlanta for auditing included the $2 million in revenue. This $2 million was not apparent in the financial reports made available to the general public, or to the RFP respondents.

The *Atlanta Journal-Constitution* reported:

> Jekyll officials say that car traffic, hotel occupancy, and convention-center business have dropped significantly the last decade. And, for the first time in years, the state park registered a deficit in fiscal 2006, according to the Jekyll Island Authority's annual report.

> It's a bleak picture. Problem is, it's not quite accurate.

> In its 2006 annual report, the Authority stated it was $210,575 in the red. But the Authority actually turned a profit of [over $1.9 million] that year,

according to the state auditor's office.

In all, the Authority's annual statements under-reported revenues by $11.3 million since fiscal 1997, according to a state auditor, John Thornton. (D. Chapman 2008)

The Jekyll Island Authority, while claiming financial duress, in 2008 signed a contract stating that for "participation in the overall revitalization development effort, JIA shall pay to L[inger] L[onger] a fee of thirty equal monthly installments of Forty Five Thousand Dollars ($45,000.00)," or over $1.3 million (Jekyll Island State Park Authority 2008). The Bleakly Advisory Group has been paid over $100,000 for its assessments, and the same amount was paid to GCI, the public relations firm hired to rebrand Jekyll Island as a vacation destination. Indeed, the financial need argument does not hold up.

As the public outcry against the Jekyll Island Authority's development plans continued through 2007, the Jekyll Island Authority persisted in making its financial case to justify new private development. In February 2008, the Jekyll Island Authority estimated it needed $50 million to cover identified capital improvement projects on the island. In August 2008, that figure rose to nearly $73 million. In February 2009, the Jekyll Island Authority claimed it needed $97.9 million for capital improvement projects, which was due to the inclusion of the convention center renovation. In a blog issued by Authority executive staff member John Hunter on March 2, 2008, the long term need for capital amounted to $500 million for the historic district alone (Hunter 2008).

The Authority's most recent list of capital improvement projects include an expansion of Summer Waves water park, paving in the campground, historic district maintenance and renovations, beach renourishment, infrastructure upgrades, and golf course redevelopment. (Note, also, that many environmental professionals recommend against beach renourishment, pointing out that it has no long-term benefit.) The need for capital improvements such as these are now given as the reason the Jekyll Island Authority must redevelop and further develop the island as a means of generating additional revenue. Yet the Authority has not accounted for how it arrived at its wish list of capital improvements. It has not prioritized these needs nor proven that the projects would be cost-effective. It also has not shown that these projects are in the best interest of the public or that they are wanted by the citizens of Georgia. At a 2009 Jekyll Island Authority board retreat, the retreat summary revealed that one participant believes a full-service spa is the greatest capital need for the historic district. I wonder if the average citizens of Georgia would say that a full service spa is on the top of their wish list for Jekyll Island's historic district. At that same retreat, it was hinted that renovations to Oleander Golf Course may require an additional $7.38 million over the $3 million currently identified as being needed.

The Authority's continuing expansion of its capital improvement needs raises a number of questions. Why was the Authority not able to say, or better yet document, how it arrived at these lists of needs? Any list of needed capital improvements should be based on a sound study of visitor experiences and preferences, not on unsubstantiated claims of need from the managing body. This is simply irresponsible and inappropriate state park management.

Regardless of the questions and protests raised from select legislators, organizations, and thousands of citizens statewide, the Jekyll Island Authority has continued, with the blessing of the state's political leadership, with its plans to bring more development and privatization to Jekyll Island State Park. In the next chapter, we will review the story of the contract between the Authority and Linger Longer Communities.

Chapter 8
The Jekyll Island Authority-Linger Longer Contract

*J.W., Hoboken, GA — Has someone been getting paid under the
table? Why is this deal so lop-sided? Who will really own Jekyll
Island in the future? Yes, Jekyll needs a face lift but it doesn't
need major reconstructive surgery! I am sure I could do a better
job of planning and do it for far less. This all just stinks.*

In Chapter 6, we traced the decade-long rush to develop Jekyll
Island. After selecting Linger Longer Communities as the
private partner, subsequent activities occurred without a signed
contract between the Jekyll Island Authority and Linger
Longer. Anxious to get a contract signed, the Jekyll Island
Authority negotiated the deal and scheduled the signing out of
the daylight of full public disclosure. The story begins in
October 2008. Senator Jeff Chapman, R-Brunswick, requested
a copy of the contract for his review. On October 27, Jekyll
Island Authority Chairman Bob Krueger promised to meet
with Senator Chapman to review the contract before it went
for Jekyll Island Authority board approval. When the senator
had heard nothing by November 24, he submitted a Georgia
Open Records Act request for a copy of the contract. To me, it

is unthinkable that a state senator should have felt forced to submit an open records request to review a contract involving a state park within his district.

On November 26, 2008 (the day before Thanksgiving), Jekyll Island Authority Executive Director Jones Hooks wrote "Confidential Memo" on an email to the Jekyll Island Authority board, confirming a December 1 board meeting. This was the meeting at which the contract with Linger Longer would be signed. The email from Hooks to the board contained information indicating that Senator Chapman had filed an open records request to review the contract (Hawkins 2008).

On that same day, Assistant Attorneys General George Zier and Denise Whiting-Pack wrote a letter to Jekyll Island Authority Chairman Bob Krueger. As required by law, Zier and Whiting-Pack had reviewed the impending contract for legal sufficiency, and were offering their review to the Authority. The two attorneys general suggested that the Authority consider a number of items.

One of their first concerns was that the Authority was moving forward with financial obligations to Linger Longer without having secured the source of funds. Zier earlier, on Monday, November 24, had expressed his concern to Whiting-Pack in an email. He said:

> FYI. Note in particular that as of Thursday, [the Jekyll Island Authority is] laying people off. And on Friday, when they say they can't afford $500,000 for program

management [to Linger Longer], so they had offered $150,000 in the "best and final offer." They end up giving $600,000 on Friday, and further obligated themselves by early starts for $350,000 in partnering payments and program management [to Linger Longer], which they have to fund themselves if bond money doesn't come through by May 1. Go figure.

Later that day, Zier sent an email to Authority Executive Director Jones Hooks questioning whether the Authority intended to give up its review of design to Linger Longer under the agreement's provisions for program management. Zier said to Hooks, "I'm not certain that providing them with such power is consistent either with the design guidelines themselves or your specific statutory mandates." According to the Information Architecture Institute, a design review "is a mechanism for ensuring design standards, alignment, and diligence throughout the course of the product design process" (2009). Zier was clearly questioning whether relinquishing such review was within the Authority's statutory authority. I cannot understand how giving up the right to review is in the public's best interest. For whom is the Jekyll Island Authority working?

Other concerns expressed by Zier and Whiting-Pack included a contract provision that allowed Linger Longer to delay construction on any asset until at least July 1, 2014, enabling them to opt out if financial conditions were unfavorable. At the same time, if the Authority completed the new convention center and infrastructure that would support Linger Longer's development by the required deadline, the Authority would be obligated to pay Linger Longer more than $1.3 million over the design and construction period. These funds were to be paid to Linger Longer for performing its "partnering obligations...and participation in the overall revitalization" (Section 5.2). In addition, the Authority would pay Linger Longer $600,000 for program management services. Zier and Whiting-Pack warned the Authority that they should ensure that the benefits to be received are worth the payments to be made.

Another concern expressed by Zier and Whiting-Pack was that during the period between November 1, 2008 and May 1, 2009 while the Authority agreed to pay Linger Longer $350,000 to be their partner, Linger Longer was obligated "only to provide a preliminary program development schedule" by January 31, 2009.

Finally, Zier and Whiting-Pack noted that under the contract provisions, Linger Longer

is *not* obligated to adhere to the quality standards of the Mobil Lodging Criteria as has been the practice of the Jekyll Island Authority during this revitalization. Instead, they are obligated to the "design and construction" standards of the lesser AAA Diamond Rating Guidelines (which are only decor, operational and services criteria) and the brand standards of a Springhill Suites, Residence Inn, Courtyard,

Fairfield Inn, or other brand of equivalent quality" (emphasis in original). In addition, Linger Longer "has *not* agreed to either work toward or attain any environmental certification or standard, such as the LEED, EarthCraft, Energy Star, or similar standards." (emphasis in original)

It appears that Assistant Attorneys General Zier and Whiting-Pack were concerned about the amount of money the Jekyll Island Authority would be obligated to pay to Linger Longer to provide services as a private sector partner, as well as the lack of obligation on Linger Longer's part to adhere to high quality lodging or environmental standards.

Of note is that many of the original financial arrangements rejected by the Jekyll Island Authority during the bid process in 2007 as being financially unsound were included in the final contract. (See figure, next page.) I have to wonder how that happened.

	Original RFP Response August 28, 2007	Revised RFP Response September 7, 2007	Revitalization Partnership Agreement December 1, 2008
Hotels	Base Rent - 8% of $350,000 per acre OR Percentage Rent: 3.5% room revenues (**excluding** food, beverage, and banquet sales)	Base Rent - 8% of $350,000 per acre OR Percentage Rent: 3.5% of **gross** revenues (**including** food, beverage, and banquet sales)	Base Rent - 6.85 % of $350,000 per acre OR Percentage Rent - 3.5% of room revenues (**excluding** food, beverage, and banquet sales for first 10 years)
Condominiums	Base Rent - 8% of $350,000 per acre 1% of purchase price contributed to Environmental Fund	Base Rent - 8% of $350,000 per acre 2% of gross sales to JIA 1% of purchase price contributed to Environmental Fund	Base Rent - $2,500 per unit per year (*To be paid by condominium owners, according to 10-15-2008 Linger Longer statement) 1% of gross sales to JIA Environmental Fund - No contribution
Timeshares (*Vacation Ownership Units*)	Base Rent - 8% of $350,000 per acre 1% of purchase price contributed to Environmental Fund	Base Rent - 8% of $350,000 per acre 2% of gross sales to JIA on new sales; 1% of resales 1% of purchase price contributed to Environmental Fund	Base Rent - $2,500 per unit per year (*To be paid by timeshare owners, according to 10-15-08 Linger Longer statement) 1% of gross sales to JIA Environmental Fund - No contribution
Partnership Contribution: Linger Longer to JIA	None	$8 million	$3.5 million
Partnership Contribution: JIA to Linger Longer	None	None	$1.35 million
Program Management Fees: JIA to Linger Longer	None	None	$600,00
Reimbursable Expenses: JIA to Linger Longer	None	None	Added 10-8-09: $600,000
LL's Investment	$360 million	$102 million	$120 million
Direct Revenue to JIA (First 15 years) excluding bond debt repayment	$102 million	$102 million	$20 million
State bond funds needed for infrastructure costs	$84.5 million	$84.5 million	$50 million

The Jekyll Island Authority-Linger Longer financial agreement evolved over time, giving the private partner an ever sweeter deal. Source: Initiative to Protect Jekyll Island

On the Friday after Thanksgiving (November 28, 2008) at approximately 4:00 p.m., the Jekyll Island Authority sent an email to Senator Chapman. The email was sent by way of his government office, which was closed for the Thanksgiving holiday. The email presented the details of the meeting that would occur the following Monday morning. This was the first communication initiated by the Jekyll Island Authority in response to Senator Chapman's October request to discuss the contract prior to signing. In that email, Senator Chapman was invited to come an hour prior to the signing to discuss the contract. Needless to say, in the middle of Thanksgiving weekend, Senator Chapman did not receive the email in time to attend on Monday morning. On the following day (Saturday, November 29, 2008), the Jekyll Island Authority publicized the upcoming meeting in the legal organ, as required. They placed the notice, however, under "Legal Notices - Miscellaneous," a category not normally used for public notices (Hawkins 2008).

The *Georgia Times-Union* reported that internal emails secured through a Georgia Open Records Request "show Authority board members were told to keep the scheduled public meeting a secret as few as five days before it was to occur" (Hawkins 2008).

Jekyll Island Authority Chairman Bob Krueger, when asked why the public was not given a chance to review the contract prior to signing, said:

> Quite frankly you can't negotiate a contract and turn around and say, "OK, John Q. Public, we've

negotiated with our partner, now what do you think?"
That's what we're for. If you did it otherwise, you're
not going to have a contract. (Hawkins 2008)

Senator Chapman, in an interview with the *Georgia
Times-Union*, said that "[The Jekyll Island Authority's
actions] show [its] contempt for the people I represent. This
is the people's business" (Hawkins 2008).

Wilson Smith, whose close following of the Jekyll Island
issue provides an interesting perspective of recent Jekyll
Island history, interviewed Senator Chapman on January 8,
2009 about the Linger Longer contract. In his podcast on
that day, Smith said:

A few weeks ago, the Jekyll Island Authority voted
to approve the contract between the Jekyll Island
Authority and Linger Longer, the revitalization partner
owned by Mercer Reynolds (Reynolds Plantation)....
Supposedly, approval of the contract was to take
place in a public meeting, but to avoid any possibility
that someone from the public might show up, the
Jekyll Island Authority held this public meeting by
phone conference. If a phone conference is a public
meeting, I am the Republican candidate for governor
in 2010.

A phone conference is one thing, but what if you were
Senator Jeff Chapman, who represents the people in
the Brunswick area, including Jekyll? In this interview

Senator Chapman details his struggle to simply get information from [the Jekyll Island Authority]. Senator Chapman is a good, honest Christian who refrains from saying bad things about people. That's all right, that's what I am here for. If I had been trying for weeks to get a copy of this contract to review and provide comments to the Jekyll Island Authority before they voted on it, if I had been told I would have an opportunity to be at the public meeting and then not been told about it, if I had found out that there were emails advising members of the Jekyll Island Authority not to tell anyone about the public meeting, if all this had happened to me, I would be in jail right now.

But, if you were Senator Chapman, you would be even more determined to stop the Jekyll Island Authority from giving away Jekyll.

The contract allowed Linger Longer to manage island amenities, such as the sixty-three holes of golf courses, the historic district, the miniature golf course, the water park, and the campground. Jekyll Island Authority Executive Director Jones Hooks acknowledged this transfer of management responsibilities to Linger Longer but protested that the Jekyll Island Authority would still retain control (Ferguson 2009a). One has to wonder, once the management of Jekyll's amenities would be handed over to Linger Longer, whether the Jekyll Island Authority would ever challenge any management decision made by this or any large private developer. One also has to wonder whether Linger Longer's management would be in the best interest of average Georgians. Of further concern is the fact that the Jekyll Island Authority Chairman Bob Krueger had stated that Linger Longer is free to make as much profit as it can from the Jekyll Island projects, as long as the Authority makes some money too (Ferguson 2009a). Such an attitude does not bode well for the future of an affordable Jekyll Island, if a private developer or a series of developers with no controls is placed in charge of the island's amenities. This policy is in direct conflict with the National Park Service's, whose directives insure that concessionaires operating in National Parks charge fees affordable to the general public.

In late 2008, Linger Longer purchased a 6,200-acre golf course community in western North Carolina. Co-owner Mercer Reynolds said of the purchase: "We are very excited to extend the *Reynolds lifestyle* to this beautiful Blue Ridge Mountain setting" (*Atlanta Business Chronicle* 2008; emphasis mine). Further, Terry Russell, president of Reynolds Signature Communities (a subsidiary of Linger Longer Communities), said, "The Reynolds name is well respected in the marketplace, and a luxury mountain community is a great compliment to what has been done at Lake Oconee" (*Atlanta Business Chronicle* 2009). A luxury community may be appropriate for privately-owned mountain or lake property, but in my mind it is hardly an appropriate model for a citizen-owned state park.

Regarding the Authority-Linger Longer contract, Jekyll Island Authority's Hooks also claimed that giving management control to Linger Longer would be "advantageous for more effective and efficient management" (Ferguson 2009a). Hooks' statement was reinforced by Authority marketing director Eric Garvey, who said that a private company overseeing public property could have an easier time making market adjustments and implementing new management practices to raise revenue. "We are held to certain guidelines and restrictions that a private company does not have," Garvey said (Ferguson 2009a). This raises two questions: Is the Jekyll Island Authority trying to circumvent the legal requirement of affordability? And what does its interpretation mean for an affordable Jekyll Island in the future?

The past, however, has proven that privatization has failed in Georgia state parks. A history of Georgia state parks stated that in the 1950s:

State government, and the parks system, [kept] trying new things to help save money. Some of the "new" things [were] simply later examples [of] ideas that had been tried before. One example of this is the concept of leasing all, or parts, of a park. Vogel and FDR [State Parks], which were leased to private operators in 1955 during the segregation era, [were] returned to state operation in 1963. Long-time Maintenance and

Operations Chief Jeff B. Naugle stated that it cost the
state almost a million dollars to get the leased parks
in good order because of the deferred maintenance
by the private operators at FDR State Park and Vogel.
Vogel had taken on the appearance of an amusement
park with pony and tram rides and miniature golf
as **facilities were developed to make money without
regard to the natural resources** (emphasis mine). FDR
had taken on a "party" atmosphere and attracted
many Fort Benning soldiers — and their lady friends.
This effort to privatize facilities was repeated in the
1990s with similar unfortunate results. (Townsend
2001, 14)....In the spring of 2001, the twenty-year
agreement with the lodge park concessionaire was
canceled after a period of four years. Privatization
of state park facilities had again failed. (Townsend
2001, 24)

The Linger Longer contract went even further, however,
than any earlier privatization of Georgia state parks. The
contract allowed the Jekyll Island Authority to "propose to
Linger Longer to acquire specific properties" on Jekyll Island
(Ferguson 2009a). To me, this is frightening. First, Linger
Longer would be allowed to operate state-owned amenities
on Jekyll Island, such as the golf and tennis complex, as if
they owned them. It seems to also mean that Linger Longer
may have purchased any amenities proposed by the Jekyll
Island Authority. We may be one step closer to another luxury

golf community, this one located in Jekyll Island State Park.

In late 2008 and early 2009, the Initiative to Protect Jekyll Island consulted with public land economist John Loomis for a professional review of the contract. Dr. Loomis, a professor at Colorado State University, is an expert in public sector economics.

Excerpts from Loomis's written review, dated January 22, 2009, are given below. These comments are somewhat technical, but understandable nonetheless. They are important because they highlight the differences between the process used by the Jekyll Island Authority and accepted professional best practices for public outdoor recreation land. As you read these comments from Dr. Loomis, consider how they fit into VEE-SIPPI, the acronym I've chosen to describe best practices in outdoor recreation planning (Visitor Experience, Environment, Science, Involvement, Park Purpose, Interdisciplinary). After each of Loomis' comments, I have added a note.

Regarding maximizing benefits to the public:

When the public (e.g., the State of Georgia, on behalf of its citizens) owns land, it is doing so with an implied "public trust" responsibility to manage the land for the benefit of the people of the state. In order to do this, a complete accounting of the full benefits and full costs of any particular action needs to be estimated and presented to decision makers and to the public. The agency should seek to maximize the net benefits (that is, the value of all benefits minus costs) to the public (Loomis and Walsh, 1997).

Note: The Jekyll Island Authority did not appear to do this at any time during the planning process. This comment touches on the best practices of understanding visitor experience, and the application of defensible scientific analysis and reporting to gain that understanding.

Regarding the private condominiums and timeshares:

A public view of public lands would suggest that it is inappropriate to sell residences to private individuals on public land. In researching and writing my book entitled *Integrated Public Lands Management* (Loomis, 1993), **I can recall no cases in the U.S. where a public land management agency currently allows individuals to purchase new private residences on public land. This essentially privatizes a portion of the public land** (emphasis mine). In the past, any private residences that were grandfathered in at the time a national park was established were typically purchased when the original owner was deceased. The Jekyll Island Authority partnership's proposed construction and sale of new private residences in a state park runs counter to the trend and conventional practice in natural resource management of parks.

Note: This comment highlights the importance of park purpose. Why was Jekyll Island State Park established? There appears to be a disconnection between the reasons for Jekyll Island's founding as the "people's park" and current management direction.

Regarding the Jekyll Island Authority's self-sufficiency mandate:

The mandate that the Jekyll Island Authority be financially self-sufficient puts the constraint on the Jekyll Island Authority that it must generate revenues sufficient to cover costs. However, as a public entity, the Jekyll Island Authority's self-sufficiency objective is NOT to maximize profits, i.e., seeking to maximize the amount of revenue in excess of costs. Revenues do not reflect the full benefit to the public and are an incomplete decision criterion for a state park agency.

Note: The Jekyll Island Authority appears to be trying to maximize profits, as if it was a private corporation. It has, as previously noted, been operating in the black for decades.

Regarding benefit-cost analyses:

Apparently no analysis has been undertaken to determine if the benefits to visitors from the additional development outweigh the costs. It is possible that visitor benefits might be increased by removing some of the older structures and NOT replacing them. But only the greater-development alternative has been proposed and investigated. Ignored are potential environmental benefits that may result from removing some of the old structures and restoring the area to a natural state. Ignored also are potential visitor benefits from creating more open, undeveloped space and associated recreational access associated with removing old structures and restoring area.

Note: This is a critical point. The Jekyll Island Authority seems to be making decisions without determining whether the benefits to Georgia citizens will be greater than the costs. From available evidence, it appears that the benefits likely do not outweigh the costs. However, no scientific cost-benefit analysis has been undertaken by the Jekyll Island Authority. In addition, the Authority has considered no other options but more beach-side development. It has tried no other way to determine whether any alternative options, including the option of "no action," would bring more benefit to the people of Georgia. Best practices in park planning require that such a range of alternatives be thoroughly evaluated.

Regarding crowding and congestion:

No analysis has been conducted of the effect on congestion and the reduction in visitor benefits from increasing visitation by twenty-one percent above previous visitation peaks and related increase in automobile traffic. An extra 100 visitors per acre of beach reduces visitor benefits by twenty-five percent (McConnell 1977). Since visitor use is projected to increase twenty-one percent beyond peak levels with the revitalization program, but the amount of beach is fixed, **the benefits each visitor receives will decrease** (emphasis mine). Given that this relationship has been available in the published literature for quite some time, and given that congestion costs are a relevant cost to the citizens of Georgia who currently visit the beach, **a complete economic analysis should have been conducted that would include this cost** (emphasis mine).

Note: I know of no study of visitor experiences on Jekyll Island conducted by the Jekyll Island Authority, including current visitor experiences or desired future experiences. You will learn about the visitation and density study done by the Bleakly Advisory Group in Chapter 10.

Regarding public input and participation:

Surveying and polling the public is a widely accepted and preferred approach to reaching an understanding of management options wanted by citizen owners of and visitors to public land. Public land management agencies often conduct surveys, sometimes in

combination with other public input approaches, to
determine public preferences for specific, different
land management and development options. Surveying
can serve to identify public benefits and costs and to
provide data for estimating them.

Note: There is not much more to be said about this. The
Jekyll Island Authority has not apparently authentically
welcomed, and has seemed, in fact, to discount public input.
To my knowledge, it has conducted no scientifically-valid
statewide surveys. Public input and involvement are two of
the important foundations of best practices in outdoor
recreation planning, and they have apparently been downplayed
by the Authority.

Regarding the public's fair return on investment:

The Jekyll Island Authority agreement indicates
that about one percent of the sale price of the town
center's condominiums and timeshares would go
to Jekyll Island Authority, with the remainder going
to the private developer. To determine if this is a
fair return to the Jekyll Island Authority, and to the
citizens of Georgia who own the beachfront property
on which these private condos and timeshares will
be located, I would look at how much of a price
premium such beachfront locations provide to the
sales price. It seems that most, if not all, of the price
premium arising from the waterfront location is due

to the public beach, not the investment of the private developer. Development of the type proposed by the developer for Jekyll Island can be located anywhere, but would bring high price premiums only at highly attractive locations, such as along the Jekyll Island beachfront. As such, most if not all the price premium could be considered a fair payment to Jekyll Island Authority and to the citizens of Georgia for use of the waterfront land.

The hedonic property model is a widely used method (Taylor and Smith 2000) for estimating the proportion of the sale price of any property, including a private residence, that is attributable to features of the property (e.g., square footage) and location (e.g., waterfront). Analysis results from using the hedonic property model show that oceanfront and waterfront price premiums can be substantial. Taylor and Smith's analysis of weekly property rentals at North Carolina beaches indicated that there is an average twenty-six percent premium for oceanfront units, as compared to those on the ocean side of an access road, but not on the oceanfront (derived from Table 7 of Taylor and Smith 2000). Thus, the state park's beach contributes as much as twenty-six percent to the price of beachside private residences. Much, if not all, of this premium would be an appropriate share to Jekyll Island Authority, *if* in fact private residences were judged by the public to be an appropriate land use (addressed above; emphasis in original).

Note: Twenty-six percent seems to be a conservative estimate of the added value of beachfront land. In Chapter 10, natural resource economist Dr. Ken Cordell provides the analysis suggested here by Dr. Loomis.

Regarding granting a price monopoly to Linger Longer Communities:

The granting of exclusive rights to develop condominiums and timeshares for sale, as well as development of hotels at a state park, provides a source of monopoly power or market power to mark up prices in excess of costs (Taylor and Smith 2000).

It is not evident that pricing guidelines limiting Linger Longer's ability to exploit its monopoly power to raise prices for condominiums and hotel rooms and earn "monopoly profits" has been set forth by the Jekyll Island Authority. Typically, National Park Service concessionaire policies involve some form of oversight on pricing to ensure that concessionaires and guides granted the exclusive right to operate in a national park do not exploit it at the expense of the visitors.

Note: To my knowledge, there has been no oversight mechanism put in place to monitor the pricing policies of

Linger Longer Communities or any private partner. In fact, the Jekyll Island Authority board has denied that such a mechanism is needed, saying that the Authority is not in the business of regulating the profits of the private sector. Professionals in the field of public land economics are not the only critics of the contract. Richard Wood, a former Jekyll Island Authority Board Chairman who helped to negotiate the first hotel redevelopment contract, said that the public return from the development is too low and Linger Longer's profits too high (Teegardin 2009). The *Atlanta Journal Constitution* conducted its own comparison of this contract with other private contracts on Jekyll Island. It found that "the authority agreed to terms [with Linger Longer] that appear more favorable than those offered in its deals with other private partners" (Teegardin 2009). It reported that Linger Longer must only pay one percent of its sale revenues to the Jekyll Island Authority, and other private partners are required to pay two percent. It also reported that Linger Longer would pocket at least $100 million while the state would get just $1.6 million from the gross sales of private timeshares and condominiums on public oceanfront land. This is a 220 percent profit after costs. From my perspective, a two percent return to the State of Georgia is grossly inadequate, but one percent is even worse. Clearly, it seems that the Jekyll Island Authority was not negotiating in the best interests of Georgia's citizens when it brokered this deal.

Wilson Smith, the attorney and former radio show host who has faithfully followed the Jekyll Island issue, was also unimpressed with the terms of the contract. Here is a transcript from one of Smith's podcasts:

> A few minutes after the broadcast of my interview with Sen. Jeff Chapman regarding the recent action of the Jekyll Island Authority, I got a phone call. It was Senator Tommie Williams, the new President Pro Tempore of the Senate. He wanted to let me know that some of the things Senator Chapman and I had discussed were not accurate. He wanted to set the record straight. I was happy to oblige.
>
> A few days later Senator Williams and I had this rather intense debate about whether or not the deal the Jekyll Island Authority had cut with Linger Longer was good or bad. Senator Williams had his figures on what the Jekyll Island Authority would be paid over the next fifteen years.
>
> My bottom line response throughout the interview was simply this: What is Linger Longer going to get out of the deal? Now, I submit that this question was imminently reasonable, that any businessman of any worth or intelligence would want to know the answer to that question before signing on the dotted line.
>
> Senator Williams did not have the figures on Linger Longer's take. His response throughout the interview was: I don't care what they make since the Jekyll

Island Authority (the State of Georgia) is getting such a good deal.

I tried to explain to the Senator that there was no way that a person could decide that the state was getting a good deal if you didn't know how much money Linger Longer was getting. I thought that made perfect sense. I thought the logic irrefutable.

Senator Williams was unconvinced. With all due respect Senator, I do not believe for one moment that you do not understand the logic of my observation. The figures of who gets how much should be the first piece of information that the Jekyll Island Authority should have at its fingertips in negotiating a contract with Linger Longer. I do not believe for a moment that Senator Williams negotiates contracts in his business without knowing exactly what benefits the other party will be getting and the monetary value of those benefits.

Senator Williams and Rep. Jerry Keen are members of the Legislative Oversight Committee that has authority over Jekyll Island. They, together with Lt. Governor Casey Cagle and lame duck Governor Perdue can fix this. All they have to do is decide they want to. No excuses. (Smith 2009b)

Senator Jeff Chapman, expressing continued concern for the contract's terms, said that "Any time you take a public asset and your statement is, 'I don't care what the private partner is making' you are saying, 'I don't know that what I am getting is fair and good for the people'" (Teegardin 2009). There is another twist to the Jekyll Island Authority-Linger Longer contract, noted previously. When the RFP for a private partner was announced and the top three candidates were identified in 2007, the Jekyll Island Authority interviewed each candidate. In their interview with Linger Longer, the Authority expressed reservations about the proposal's financial terms. Specifically, in an August 28, 2007 question and answer session with Linger Longer regarding its proposal, the Jekyll Island Authority stated:

> The financial return to [the] Jekyll Island Authority as presented in your proposal does not seem at all commensurate with the level of upfront public investment required and the long range financial benefit to Linger Longer from the development. We could not recommend the financial return to [the] Jekyll Island Authority's Board as sound financial stewardship for the future of Jekyll Island.

Linger Longer responded by softening the financial terms of their proposal and was selected as the Authority's private partner. When the agreement was finally signed by the partners in December 2008, however, the terms had again changed, giving Linger Longer a much sweeter financial deal in spite of the fact that the revised development plans had been scaled back. The $1.3 million, mentioned previously as a payment to Linger Longer just to be the private partner, was added to the agreement. Linger Longer had agreed, following its interview with the Authority, to cover a portion of the infrastructure costs. These costs were now being entirely borne by the citizens of Georgia in the form of General Obligation Bonds. The signed agreement of 2008 does not match the financial terms, even on a proportional basis, laid out in the proposal that was approved in 2007. Linger Longer, in summary, was getting a proportionally better deal now than they would have, had the original proposal remained in force (See figure on page 144).

The $50 million in state-backed bonds to provide the infrastructure for Linger Longer's town center project also included a new "signature park" and convention center on Jekyll Island. Senator Eric Johnson, an ex-officio member of the Jekyll Island Authority board, helped to secure these bonds. Recall that Senator Johnson's campaign manager, in his bid to become Governor, is Jamie Reynolds, a principal in Linger Longer Communities (McDonald 2009, Morekis 2009). Repayment of those bonds will cost taxpayers roughly $100 million (Chapman 2009).

In response to the approval of the state bonds, Senator Chapman proposed to his legislative colleagues that they require the Jekyll Island Authority to renegotiate a fairer contract with Linger Longer, perhaps by splitting the profits equally rather than by ninety-nine percent to one percent. No action was taken on Chapman's proposal.

On April 1, 2009, the *Atlanta Journal Constitution* ran the following short news story about the waning days of the 2009 legislative session:

> Sen. Robert Brown (D-Macon) tried to make a point on how the state spends money during final passage of the state 2010 budget Wednesday. He pitted money for Jekyll Island development against money for sick veterans.
>
> Brown offered an amendment that would take out $2.14 million meant for Jekyll Island and give it to the Milledgeville domiciliary unit of the Georgia War Veterans Home.
>
> Eighty-one veterans, all with health problems, lived at the domiciliary unit, which the Georgia Department of Veterans Affairs closed because of budget cuts.
>
> The state did find money in the budget to help a politically-connected development company with plans to redevelop Jekyll Island. Legislators have put money in the budget to pay to upgrade the island convention center and build an ocean-side park as part of the project. The developers plan to replace older buildings along the beachfront with new hotels and condos.
>
> Brown's amendment failed and the budget passed.

Public response to the failure of Brown's amendment provides a clue as to how angry Georgia citizens had become over the Jekyll Island-Linger Longer deal. "Disgusted" posted this response to the *Atlanta Journal Constitution* article:

The senators of Georgia who voted against this amendment should be ashamed of themselves. They have put their own self interest and need to follow the party line BEFORE caring for the men and women who served our country. I wonder how they will answer their children and grandchildren when asked what they were most proud of in their time as a senator…the answer will not be voting against this amendment, that is, if they are men and women of any moral character.

In the meantime, the Jekyll Island Authority moved forward, apparently still without public input or participation. (Recall that public involvement is one of the primary foundations of accepted outdoor recreation planning.) Examination of the Jekyll Island Authority-Linger Longer contract revealed that an updated convention center and a new public park are two of the capital projects the Jekyll Island Authority must begin before Linger Longer could move forward.

I will close this chapter on the Jekyll Island Authority-Linger Longer contract with a prophetic quote from a Wilson Smith podcast from April 1, 2008:

If you have been paying attention to the controversy

over the planned development of the beach at Jekyll Island, you will want to know that Senator Jeff Chapman's efforts to get the legislature to do something (anything really) to limit development of the beach have been rebuffed by the gurus of development-at-all-cost.... There is just too much money going to be made by Linger Longer, Mercer Reynolds and good ole...contributors to Governor Perdue to let this gold mine get stopped by something as silly as the will of the people of Georgia. I have a lot of respect for [Republican] Senator Chapman who seems to be focused on trying to do what is right.

The Revised Revitalization Partnership Agreement

In the fall of 2009, it became known that revisions to the Jekyll Island Authority-Linger Longer contract were in the works. If this revised contract was signed by December 14, 2009, Linger Longer's deal would get even sweeter. The revised terms called for an additional $700,000 in "management fees," making the cost of doing business with Linger Longer nearly $3 million. And, this upfront money was on top of the more than $100 million profits to be made by Linger Longer Communities on round one of the Jekyll land deal.

Chapter 9
The Jekyll Island Authority Begins to Fulfill
Its Contract with Linger Longer

C.P., Athens, GA — I love Jekyll and DO NOT want it to change. I love the naturalness of it and the historical aspects, the beauty and serenity. I love to come there to relax. I feel safe by myself (a single woman). I can ride my bike for miles, walk on the beach, enjoying all the beautiful scenery, and feel almost like I am at my own private island. The beach is natural, with no hotels lined up, no wall to wall people, noise and all that ugliness. I need a place like Jekyll, I crave the visit to Jekyll! I feel a special love for it. Please, please don't let greedy, self serving, callous and clueless humans (?) destroy my paradise. I am far from a rich person, but I can manage to get to Jekyll every so often to soothe my soul.

One of the requirements for moving forward with the Jekyll Island Authority-Linger Longer contract was the selection of a firm to "provide planning, architectural and engineering services for an overhaul of the island's outdated convention center and design of the proposed beachfront park" (Ferguson 2009b). On March 9, 2009 at the Jekyll Island Authority board meeting, Executive Director Jones Hooks discussed the selection of an architectural firm to accomplish this.

The selection committee's top choice was approved and on March 11, 2009, the *Brunswick News* reported that the Jekyll Island Authority had chosen Helman, Hurley, Charvat & Peacock (HHCP) Architects to begin work. Their task was to design the public areas of the newly dubbed "beach village." On July 14, the newspaper reported on the firm's new plans for Jekyll Island. In an email response to a Georgia Open Records Act request on August 13, 2009, Executive Director Jones Hooks told me that public input on this part of the plan had been "ongoing for the last year and a half." I wondered, as involved as I thought I had been in the Jekyll Island development process, how had I completely missed this opportunity for public input.

The concept provided by HHCP was more encompassing than expected. The firm, after reviewing the conceptual design for Linger Longer's town center and adjacent hotels, timeshares, and condominiums, presented a concept that included a revised vision for the entire area. The new concept plan was welcomed by residents and other citizens, as its approach was more visually appealing and it downplayed the commercial components to be built and managed by Linger Longer Communities. The site, however, while more visually appealing, still contained the condominiums and timeshares opposed by Georgia citizens.

According to the Initiative to Protect Jekyll Island:

The basics are that Jekyll will have a new entry road that will feed into a roundabout overlooking a village green and a pedestrian shopping area with an open view of the beach. To the north of that area will be a new, enlarged convention center and a beach park that will include changing stations, rest rooms, picnic facilities, a beachfront promenade, and dune crossovers. To the south will be two hotels and a 160-unit time-share complex. Seventy-five condos are in the plan as loft units above the retail shops. Construction is scheduled to begin by the end of this year and to be completed in 2012. (2009a)

What I found disturbing about this process is that I could find no public notification about the bid or selection process. Nor could I find any call for citizen input or participation. Fortunately for the citizen-owners of Jekyll Island State Park, the concept plan presented by HHCP appeared to address some of the public's concerns expressed over the previous three years. A more citizen-friendly concept plan for Jekyll Island State Park, however, does not excuse the apparent continued exclusion of the public that seems to define the Jekyll Island Authority's business-as-usual approach to decision-making.

After the concept plan had been made public, the Jekyll Island Authority felt that it could move forward with plans for the new retail section of the beach village. According to Jekyll Island Authority Executive Director Jones Hooks, "Linger Longer has a responsibility for looking at the retail component and deciding what the retail mix needs to be.

[The Jekyll Island Authority is] not necessarily in control of all that" (Hawkins 2009b). In other words, a private development company, known for its upscale lakefront residential development and the "Reynold's Lifestyle," had been placed in control of what kind of shopping would be possible at a Georgia state park. And the Jekyll Island Authority responded to the public as if the decision to give Linger Longer control of Jekyll's retail configuration was out of their hands. If not the Authority, who was making the decisions about what happens in Jekyll Island State Park?

The uncertainty and apparent lack of Jekyll Island Authority control has made some of the current retailers

Jekyll's home-grown businesses have served island visitors for decades.

uncomfortable about their future on the island. The owner of Maxwell's Hardware and Variety Store and the IGA grocery, both in operation since 1973, stated: "I just want to be included in the plans" (Hawkins 2009b).

But being included is not something upon which small business owners can depend. The home-grown businesses that have been serving Jekyll Island visitors, some for decades, must make a decision. Should they want to continue in business on Jekyll Island until the new retail center is completed, they are being required to relocate to trailers for the next two to five years. The Jekyll Island Pharmacy, as a result, closed its doors on December 31, 2009.

In an email dated December 25, 2009, Jekyll resident Howard Sculthorpe outlined the situation as he saw it, after conferring with one of the Jekyll business owners. He determined that the small businesses on Jekyll, should they choose to remain during the construction period, will need to move at least twice. Each move will cost in terms of transferring merchandise, as well as down time with no sales. Even if they make this commitment, they have no assurance that they will be included in the new retail center. And if they get to stay, the Jekyll Island Authority has not shared their rental rate with them. Sculthorpe asked why the Jekyll Island Authority does not:

1. Direct the preliminary design of the new retail center with input from the current small business owners who have been on Jekyll for years?

2. Set and communicate a fee structure to help the small business owners make a decision about whether they could afford to operate in the new retail center?

3. Ask for commitments from business owners willing to do business on Jekyll?

According to the *Florida Times Union*:

Jekyll Pharmacy owner John Waters, who has been in business on Jekyll for 35 years, said he will close his store at the end of December (2009) rather than move into a trailer. A double-wide would have cut his floor space by two-thirds. It's not enough room to sell the volume he needs to turn a profit, he said.

"I'm too old and the store's not going to be saleable through this transition," said Waters, 65 (Hawkins 2009a).

The retail situation continued to change throughout the fall of 2009, causing even more uncertainty among Jekyll's small business owners. Again, from the *Florida Times Union*:

Linger Longer, as the park's revitalization partner, was also supposed to rebuild the retail center, as well as other buildings in the beach village. The construction schedule was due in December, but an October contract amendment got the company off the hook.

The new agreement now splits the retail project into two parts. The state will pay for and build half of the retail complex, for essential services like the grocery store, bank, pharmacy and post office, while Linger Longer is "entitled to build" an as-yet undetermined additional amount of commercial space.

Jekyll Realty owner C.J. Jeffries said he's not sure if his business qualifies as "essential" or who his new landlord will be. Still, he'll likely commit to a two-year trailer lease by the authority's Dec. 15 [2009] deadline.

"It's in our best interests to find some way to go forward, because our company manages vacation rentals on Jekyll Island. Maintaining a presence here is vital," he said.

Still, Jeffries said he would like some assurances his business will have a future on Jekyll.

"I've asked if we could have first rights of refusal on any new space, but that's been put on hold because we still don't know who the builder is going to be," he said. "I would like some kind of pledge that we'll get first crack at this. The alternative is to get squeezed out of business."

Zachry's Seafood Restaurant, operating on Jekyll for

thirty-five years, will relocate to an exit of off I-95. This hardly seems like the way to reward Jekyll's small entrepreneurs, the business owners who have provided goods and services to Jekyll's visitors for decades. According to Hawkins (2009a), business owners said they need to know what will happen at least a year in advance to properly plan for their businesses. But demolition of the current retail center is set for June 2010, and the local businesses remain unsure of their future. According to one of the businessowners, "[The JIA] can't answer any questions. I wish they would be clear [about what will happen]."

Changes in the retail mix will not be the only transformation evident on Jekyll Island. On September 22, 2009, the Georgia Department of Transportation sent an interdepartmental letter to the Division of Intermodal Programs, informing them of an upgrade to the Jekyll Island airport. The majority of the funds ($375,000) for this upgrade will come from the federal government, and the state's taxpayers will pay almost nine thousand dollars for this project. I wonder how many of the state's taxpayers will benefit from Jekyll Island's new and improved airport?

The Jekyll Island Authority's Annual Financial Statement

At the March 9, 2009 board meeting, the Jekyll Island Authority's Finance Chairman Mike Hodges reported lower than expected revenues for the year ending February 2009. Some of this, according to Executive Director Hooks, was related to the global economic downturn. The figures cited by Mr. Hodges, however, did not reflect an added expense incurred by the Jekyll Island Authority by virtue of its contract with Linger Longer. At the meeting, resident and IPJI Co-director David Egan inquired whether the cited figures included the $45,000 being paid monthly to Linger Longer just to be the private partner. Director Jones Hooks replied that they did not; and further, the Jekyll Island Authority was accruing the financial obligation to Linger Longer rather than paying it. The accumulation of debt, in my own experience, does not erase one's obligation to pay it. This is true whether it is you, me, or the Jekyll Island Authority. At some time in the future, the Jekyll Island Authority would be required to pay the $1.3 million to Linger Longer, just for being its private partner. For every dollar paid to Linger Longer just to be the private partner, there would be one less dollar available to restore Jekyll's native ecosystems, improve or extend its bike trails, improve interpretive services, or support additional park staff.

In May 2009, IPJI Co-director and Jekyll resident Mindy Egan requested a copy of the Jekyll Island Authority's 2008 annual report. In an email sent to me on June 3, 2009, Egan reported that she was informed by the Authority that because it was engaged in an "increased number of on-going public communications over the past year," an annual report would be "nothing more than a rehash of this material" (Egan 2009). It would, therefore, no longer be published. This action, in effect, reduces the Jekyll Island Authority's public accountability even more, as citizens must now piece together information from numerous communications to understand the Authority's income and expenses by category over the previous twelve months. In the past, the board's annual reports have drawn criticism for presenting a misleading picture of the Authority's financial health. It is no wonder the Jekyll Island Authority wants less, rather than more, public accountability.

On June 2, 2009, the *Georgia Times-Union* reported that "a typographical error on a newly signed hotel contract will lower Jekyll Island State Park revenues by $90,000 per year unless it is fixed" (Hawkins 2009c). Although acknowledging that losing that much revenue for the next fifty years would "be a real hit for us," Jekyll Island Authority Executive Director Jones Hooks felt that the mistake could be corrected. For everyone's sake, let's hope that is true. Although mistakes happen, one has to wonder why the contract with the Jekyll Oceanfront Resort was not more carefully scrutinized by the reportedly cash-strapped Jekyll Island Authority prior to signing.

In July 2009, the Jekyll Island Authority board voted to increase the daily entrance fee from three to five dollars. This increase is larger than it first appears, since it will apply for every day a visitor is on the island. This recent increase mirrored a similar increase in all state park entrance fees statewide. The Jekyll Island Authority, however, has often claimed that Jekyll Island is not in the state park system, since it is operated by an Authority. Suddenly, the Authority decided that they had no choice but to follow the state park system's new policy. In an editorial written July 15, 2009, the *Brunswick News* stated:

[The Jekyll Island Authority voted to raise entry fees] after the taxpayers of the state just guaranteed loans of $25 million for infrastructure improvements that will facilitate new development on Jekyll Island that Georgians will see, if all goes well, in 2012. Now, the [Jekyll Island Authority] board might be asked, how many state parks are getting that?

That's not all Jekyll Island is getting from taxpayers. It's also receiving thousands in sales tax dollars that are generated in Glynn County - tax dollars that could be used for city and county projects instead of state projects. That's something else no other state park in Georgia is getting.

Jekyll Island is feeling the sting of a weak economy. It believes the five dollar entrance fee is necessary to offset its losses.

But why should it take the one step - raise prices - that every economist on...planet Earth would recommend against when business is bad?

The editorial further noted that while visitors may continue to come to Jekyll Island, the higher fee may cause them to be more frugal in their spending while on the island. Again, the Jekyll Island Authority had the opportunity to solicit public input on this matter. Had it done so, its decision would be based on solid information from visitors, rather than appearing to be arbitrary and profit-seeking, as if it were a business and not a state park.

Revelations from the Jekyll Island Authority Board Retreat

On June 17–18, 2009, the Jekyll Island Authority board convened a retreat to provide a vision for Jekyll Island State Park's future. Board members and Jekyll Island Authority Executive Director and department heads attended the retreat. No average citizens were invited. A number of concerns surfaced over the two-day meeting, held in Smarr, Georgia. One apparent concern was for the upcoming 2010 legislative session and gubernatorial election. For example, one participant said that "We need to make plans that ensure buildings start being built prior to the next legislative session," and another: "Gubernatorial race possibly making JI a politicized sacrificial lamb" (Jekyll Island Authority 2009). One strategy discussed to address this concern was the need for a briefing with all gubernatorial candidates to provide a status report on Jekyll's "revitalization."

Participants expressed more immediate concerns as well. For example, one "pressing issue" regarded the $25 million in state bond funds approved by the 2009 General Assembly: "[The] possibility of a Special Legislative Session in August that could jeopardize the $50 million bond deal," and "We must be moving forward with our plans to assure that the additional $25 million in bonds for Jekyll Island are part of the fall state bond sale — if not, the second $25 million of bonds could be threatened by budget deficits" (Jekyll Island Authority 2009). (The $50 million in General Obligation Bonds has remained intact and is now being used to build a new park and in the near future, a new convention center.)

One participant expressed a surprising pressing concern: "Jekyll Island Authority discussed a fall-back plan of other private partners should Linger Longer not follow through on commitments." In light of the events that happened six months later, this comment seems to indicate that the Linger Longer-Jekyll Island Authority private-public partnership had already begun to falter. Other items discussed included the need to support the Jekyll Island Authority-Glynn County relationship, since "the Jekyll Island Authority may need to request a greater percentage of SPLOST funds to help pay for beach re-nourishment and other capital projects that have county-wide impact." The retreat summary revealed that at least one participant felt that "the greatest need at the Jekyll Island Club Hotel is for a full service spa." The attendees also identified a need to meet with representatives from the Department of Natural Resources to "ensure that the Shore Protection permit is successful." In 2008, Linger Longer was forced to redesign its plans for the town center after it became clear that the state would not provide an exemption to build in the Shore Protection Zone. The new permit being sought was needed to build Jekyll Island's "Signature Park," which is required by the Jekyll Island Authority-Linger Longer contract. This park, however, will be financed by Georgia citizens through State General Obligation Bonds.

One attendee, when asked what he or she would see in fifteen years on Jekyll Island, replied that "we're sitting at the new casino on Jekyll Island" (Jekyll Island Authority 2009). Clearly, this individual has a different vision for the future of Jekyll Island State Park than I and thousands of citizens.

Under the category of "Privatization of Enterprise Operations," the retreat summary stated that

> the management and operation of the golf courses should be put out for bid (Linger Longer gets first right of refusal). Given the estimated $11 million cost of renovating Oleander [golf course], members of the Jekyll Island Authority stated that it may make more sense to pursue the development of some golf villas around the courses on existing real estate. The Jekyll Island Authority would like to pursue a public-private partnership for condo or villa development in association with the golf courses within the next five years (Jekyll Island State Park Authority 2009).

It appears that the Jekyll Island Authority will not rest after the beachside complex, with its two hotels, a retail center, and private condominiums and timeshares, has been developed. It seems that the Jekyll Island Authority's answer to every question is the development of more hotels, privately-owned condominiums and timeshares, and now golf course villas, in our state park.

The Proposed Jekyll Island Residential Lease Policy

On July 21, 2009, the Bleakly Advisory Group completed another no-bid analysis for and report to the Jekyll Island Authority. This time, the Bleakly Group analyzed and recommended a new residential lease policy. This analysis was apparently undertaken, once again, without the benefit of public participation. The firm examined eight settings across the United States; none of the eight were comparable as none were on state park land. The Authority was apparently concerned that residential leases have not been tied to the market, and therefore the income gained from the leases is far below where it should be for island property. The obvious question, from my perspective, is why the Jekyll Island Authority was so concerned about increasing its income from long-time island residents, while at the same time giving Linger Longer Communities such generous terms on publicly-owned beachfront acreage being operated for private corporate profit.

I believe one of the more troubling paragraphs in the Bleakly Advisory Group's report is found under "Recommendations:"

Over time, the Jekyll Island Authority should attempt to build a reserve fund, **and/or work with its revitalization partners to buy back residential leaseholds on the island as properties become available for resale** (emphasis mine). Current lease holders who do not wish to extend their leases will see their properties return to the Authority at the end of the lease term in 2049. Thus, at a minimum the Authority will have the option of re-leasing these properties upon lease termination. In certain cases, the present value of future cash flow to the Jekyll Island Authority from restructuring and re-leasing parcels could exceed the purchase price. **Selective acquisitions and investments can also be used strategically by the Jekyll Island Authority to encourage private reinvestment where needed.** (Bleakly Advisory Group 2009a, 39; emphasis mine)

My concern is that this is opening the door to further corporate ownership and development of Jekyll Island State Park.

Chapter 10
A Professional Opinion about Smoke and Mirrors
By Ken Cordell, PhD

V.S., Atlanta, GA — Jekyll Island is unique and rich in history. Let's protect that and not create yet another island which becomes a profit center for developers who don't appreciate what currently exists!

S.O., Rome, GA — Please keep Jekyll Island free of luxury housing and hotels that would destroy the environment and the opportunity to enjoy nature. There are places the world over to take care of the wealthy, while there are fewer and fewer places for people with average incomes.

I have been in the field of parks and recreation for over thirty-five years. I was taught, and subsequently taught others, that public service means giving first, last, and all in-between considerations to the public. Managing public land is an outstanding example of public service. The public service emphasis in properly managing public land is always that of serving visitors and protecting the park. But in following closely for the last three years the unfolding story of Jekyll

Island, *our* state park, I have come to see that perhaps not all who are charged with responsibly managing public land see their charge the way I do. In fact, never in my thirty-five plus years of public service have I seen a greater apparent lack of concern about the public interest than in the way planning for the future of Jekyll Island State Park has proceeded. This is, of course, my perception as one who is on the outside of the decision process. But I am not alone in being outside. All citizen-owners of this priceless state park are outside because the decision process is a closed one, not open to professional or public scrutiny.

As I read the analysis reports apparently guiding decision making, the metaphor of smoke and mirrors, as in the Wizard of Oz, came to mind. With an emphasis on revenues, commercial development and profits, the reports bore but a smoky or fuzzy resemblance to the true purposes of state parks. All the "right words" were reflected in press releases and official communications, but behind the mirror the emphasis was on revenue potentials and commercial development. These are not the true purposes of state parks.

My research over the years has clearly shown that public lands, especially state parks, are of high value to the citizens of Georgia. In fact, parks are important to all Americans. Just think what state parks would sell for if put on the market to the highest bidder (heaven forbid). Just think what the capitalized value of state parks in Georgia would be if all the memorable experiences of all future generations of visitors were added up over the next 250 years and their present worth calculated.

Ironically, and as unnerving as it may sound, for many of our public parks, there is a looming challenge almost as threatening as selling them. That challenge is whether some, or even all, of the operations, facilities and occupancy rights for these parks will be privatized, commercially developed, and made into profit-making enterprises. Public parks, such as Jekyll, are highly desirable. They are usually very scenic, have abundant wildlife, offer an existing visitor base, are well known, and are rich in natural amenities.

In this chapter I will attempt to clear away some of the smoke and mirrors that seem to have shrouded decisions about Jekyll Island State Park's future. First, I provide a brief overview of how a professional planner would proceed with park planning. As we will see, park planning properly done emphasizes, of all things, listening to, engaging, and being entirely open to the people who own the park (citizens, that is). Second, I will attempt to clear some of the smoke surrounding what perhaps has been one of the most controversial issues, which is the assertion that visitation to Jekyll Island has plunged since the mid-1990s. This "plunge" smoke screen seems to have been the primary basis for the conclusion on the Authority's part that only commercial development could save the state park.

Third I will take a look at the analysis to project future costs and revenues associated with planned commercial operations and development. With this, the smoke thickened and an ever-increasing list of costly, "essential" capital improvements emerged. Fourth, I will examine the "density study" that looked at the impacts of development on the density of housing, visitors and developed space. This "density study" proceeded by comparing the density of visitors, residents, and housing envisioned for Jekyll with other developed Atlantic Coast islands. As we will see, with completion of the density study the smokiness of the decision process increased.

Finally, in this chapter, an economic comparison is made between the financial terms given one of the contracted private developers (Linger Longer Communities) and what the scientific, published real estate economics literature indicates such terms should be. This comparison contrasts the profit-sharing terms the Jekyll Island Authority approved in its December, 2008, contract with Linger Longer with what those profit-sharing terms could have been if an appropriate, best-science economics approach had been taken. Also offered in that last section of this chapter is an economic analysis to show what rent the developer should pay the citizen-owners of Jekyll Island for development rights on park land (if such a thing is bound to be allowed). By citizen-owners I mean the taxpayers, i.e., the citizens who own Jekyll Island. Since the writing of this chapter, Linger Longer Communities has withdrawn from its contract with Jekyll Island Authority. But since the Authority has said it intends to pursue its commercial development agenda nonetheless, the economic analysis I offer is still appropriate, if not more so now.

Proper Public Park Planning

Public parks, such as state parks, have as their primary purposes the provision of quality park experiences for users and protection of park cultural and natural resources. To achieve these purposes, proper park planning processes must be understood and employed. Proper public park planning is an open, participatory, and collaborative process. Properly done, there are no secrets, no closed meetings, and no surprise announcements of contracts. Citizens are encouraged to help define the vision for how their parks will be used and managed. Citizens are intimately involved from the very beginning. A rich and extensive literature exists documenting how and why public park planning principles work (e.g., Driver 1999; Litman 2007; Loomis 2002). Professionally-based park planning must thoroughly consider the costs, benefits, and distributional effects of management options, and as well the tradeoffs and effects on natural systems. Professional associations which strongly endorse the philosophies and principles of public service planning include the American Planning Association, the National Planning Association, and the National Governors' Association.

A recent release of planning principles by the National Association of Recreation Resource Planners puts it plainly. All park and recreation planning includes the following (paraphrased by this author):

- Undertake comprehensive public and stakeholder collaboration to identify recreation and tourism demand, public issues, management concerns, unique opportunities, threats to the resource, and equity concerns.

- Openly establish the planning and decision criteria to be used for identifying and evaluating management alternatives.

- Inventory the resource and evaluate uses and pressures using the best available methods, science, and information.

- With the public fully engaged, formulate alternatives which address the significant demands, issues, concerns, opportunities, and threats. No action is a viable alternative.

- Evaluate the consequences, benefits, and effects of each proposed alternative using the best available data and sciences.

- Select a preferred alternative based upon a full and reasoned analysis and upon solid support from stakeholders and the public.

- Implement the preferred alternative and monitor its implementation using appropriate indicators of both social and resource costs and benefits.

- Modify the plan as needed and assure the public is involved in all phases of execution and modification.

An adequate public park planning process addresses all significant public issues, management concerns, opportunities, and threats. In doing so, recreation planning requires consideration of many inputs. Some of these inputs include existing plans and policies, current type and amount of recreation use, overall recreation demand trends, visitor and stakeholder preferences, and related public issues. Other inputs include management concerns, regional supply of recreation opportunities, economic impact of recreation participation, best available science, environmental conditions, and any other relevant information. Sound recreation resource planning engages, hears from, and is responsive to all the diverse publics who value the recreation resource. Each alternative can be contrasted by the following: (1) its proposed objectives; (2) desired future conditions; (3) desired recreation experiences, facilities, management strategies, and actions; (4) quality standards; (5) visitor capacities; (6) economic value; (7) projected budget requirements; and (8) monitoring program. The analytical stage in a planning process is the evaluation of alternatives whereby the alternatives should be sharply contrasted, and the pros and cons are rigorously evaluated so the reasons for and against each alternative become clear.

In the following sections of this chapter, I attempt to see through what appear to me as three smoky examples of the type of analysis and information used by the Jekyll Island Authority in reaching decisions to move forward aggressively with commercial development. Following these examples, a mirror is held up to the profit-sharing and beach-front rental rate terms given to Linger Longer by the Jekyll Island Authority. It will be interesting to see if a clear image of public trust shows in the mirror's reflection.

1. A Claim that Visitation to Jekyll Island Declined by Almost One-Half in One Year

In most citizens' view, commercial development does not belong in state parks, except for lodges, cabins, rustic restaurants, and camp stores. For Jekyll Island, however, downward trending visitation was drifted out initially as the primary justification for needing new hotels, a new convention center, new commercial space, and hundreds of private timeshares and condominiums in Jekyll Island State Park.

Annual estimates of visitation to Jekyll Island have been based loosely on records of incoming vehicle traffic and an assumed number of people in each vehicle (which has never been adequately documented). There were two sources for monitoring incoming traffic to Jekyll Island. One was the Georgia Department of Transportation (GA DOT) and their statewide traffic monitoring system. This system uses a light traffic flow sample for any one highway alone, such as the causeway to the island. The other source was the recorded number of vehicles entering Jekyll Island at the park entrance booth. Based on interpretations of these sources, the Authority claimed that traffic, and thus visitation to the Park, declined over forty-seven percent in just a few years. They claimed that most of this occurred in just one year, between 1996 and 1997.

Visitation measures the number of recreation visits during a period, usually over a one-year period. Very different interpretations on my part and others of the DOT and Jekyll Island Authority traffic flow records have led to very different interpretations of recreation visitation trends as reported by the Jekyll Island Authority. Admittedly, estimating visitation at a public park is tricky, even for one with only a single entrance. I have done a great deal of research in this area and know this to be the case. When one encounters anomalies in the data, however, one looks for lines of evidence by which to double check the likely reality of the estimates produced. This was the approach I took when first given the opportunity to examine the visitation trend being reported by the Jekyll Island Authority. The decline in visitation claimed by the Jekyll Island Authority and by the Bleakly Advisory Group was shown as having occurred mostly during a single year, between 1996 and 1997 (see the top line in the graph on page 192).

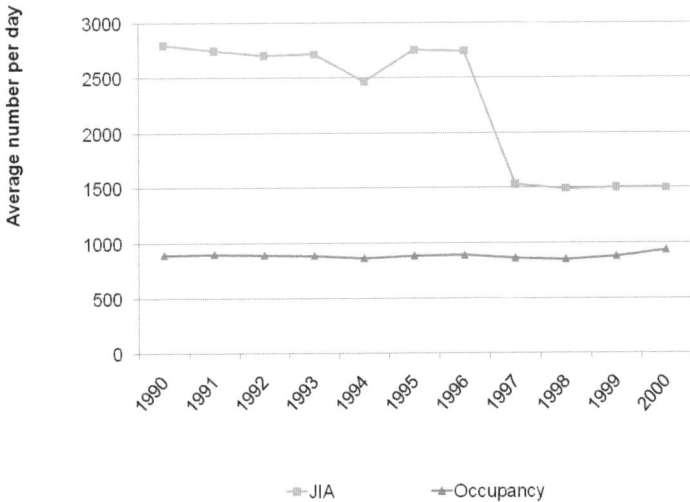

-■-JIA　　　　-▲-Occupancy

Average number of entering vehicles (Jekyll Island Authority original traffic data) and average number of hotel rooms occupied at Jekyll Island State Park, 1990-2000.

Such a drastic decline in just one year's time as one sees in the top line is highly unusual for park visitation. I looked at two things in an attempt to understand how visitation to Jekyll Island could plunge as much as was reported. One thing looked at was the trend in the DOT traffic estimates on the causeway. These estimates were based on two-day counts at different seasons of the year (a 0.005% sample). The DOT never designed its sampling to provide annual traffic flow estimates for a single road in a network of roads. Knowing something about sampling traffic flows to park and recreation areas, I adjusted the DOT traffic estimates to reflect time-of-year sampling differences. After adjustment, the DOT estimates failed to confirm the Jekyll Island Authority's reported large drop in vehicles, and therefore visitation.

A second point of investigation was the trend in daily number of hotel rooms occupied for the years 1990 to 2000 (the bottom line in the graphic above). If visitation had plummeted drastically as reported, then hotel room occupancy should have reflected that plummet. However, hotel room occupancy across these years of reported visitation decline varied very little. Like the GA DOT traffic data examination, this other source of evidence failed to substantiate the reported dramatic visitation decline. The Jekyll Island Authority has claimed that visitation, golf rounds, and convention attendance has continued to drop over the last several years. However, what one does not hear the Jekyll Island Authority say is that hotels were allowed to become "run down" and that a number of them have been demolished recently. Loss of hundreds of hotel rooms must surely have been the largest factor in determining visitation decline. Yet, there has been no admission that declining visitation has been affected by allowing hotels to deteriorate to the point they had to be torn down and contracted for replacement.

2. The Bleakly Advisory Group, the Smoking Capital Improvements List, and Revenue Projections

In late 2008, the Bleakly Advisory Group (contracted consultant to the Authority) presented an update of its development impact study, as commissioned by the Jekyll Island Authority. To me this analysis by the Bleakly Advisory Group and the Jekyll Island Authority once again missed the mark. Again, the analysis did not use the proper criteria for state park planning. Proper criteria are quality visitor experiences (emphasis on visitors — not on accommodating permanent residents) and protection of park resources. The stated overall purpose of the Bleakly Advisory Group analysis was to quantify the economic, transportation, visitation, cost, and revenue effects of proposed development. No alternative to development was considered.

The Bleakly development analysis looked at:

1. The characteristics of Jekyll Island's "build out"

2. Correlations between development patterns and the island's roads, water, sewer, and electrical infrastructure

3. Listing capital expenditures and the island's capacity to accommodate more development

4. Forecast of revenues

As the Bleakly Advisory Group's impact analysis progressed, the Jekyll Island Authority proceeded to grow a list of "needed" capital improvements. The list grew from about $50 million in February 2008, to over $70 million in late 2008, then to over $100 million by early 2009. There is some indication that the list (and dollar amounts) keeps growing, with the Jekyll Island Authority recently suggesting a figure as high as $500 million (Hunter 2008). This growing list of capital improvements and shortfalls in revenues were cited as the primary reasons commercial development of the park was essential. No justifications for any of the items on the lists, nor any analysis of the cost of these items was ever made public to my knowledge.

The Jekyll Island impact analysis was shared with members of the private consulting teams and with the Jekyll Island Authority. To my knowledge, it was not shared willingly with the public, or with representatives of the public. Only through Georgia Open Records Act requests for documents did any detailed information come to light. I am not aware either that anyone of the public or visitors was asked to help develop the "wish lists." The Bleakly Advisory Group and Jekyll Island Authority impact assessment process could have been greatly improved and made non-controversial by adopting an open, public participatory process in the beginning. Adoption of openness could especially have been helpful in looking at impacts of development on "visitor experiences." Who better to evaluate impacts on visitor experiences than visitors? Instead, a consulting company that admittedly had no one on staff with park and recreation training or professional affiliation was contracted to evaluate impacts of commercial development on visitor experiences. Professional research clearly indicates that different visitors will have quite different expectations of what constitutes satisfying park experiences. Thus far, visitors have not been given the appropriate opportunity to define the future of their state park.

To my knowledge, other than commercial development, no alternative park future scenarios were considered. For example, one scenario that should have been considered is "no new development" beyond replacement of the run down hotels and convention center. Under this scenario, the Authority could allow nature to take its course by letting the beach migrate naturally as north to south beach movement continues. Consequently, many of the items on the capital improvements list could simply have been eliminated. Based on overviews in the 2004 Park Master Plan Update and on the 2007 Park Conservation Plan, Jekyll Island is admired by visitors for what it is now, especially for its naturalness and support of wildlife. Instead, the Jekyll Island Authority is hoping for a twenty percent increase in annual visitation to a level of 2.65 million. Unless I overlooked it, there was apparently no state-of-the-art visitation forecasting model developed or submitted for peer review as professional planners would have done. There was no apparent accounting for potential beach crowding or wildlife impacts. There also seemed to be no accounting for possible displacement of some segments of the current visitor base (which is well documented in the literature).

The projected cost of items on the capital improvements needs list included both added infrastructure expansion and major debt servicing. In fact, debt servicing was shown as approximately two-thirds of the total annual growth in revenues projected as needed starting sometime after 2012. Taking a different approach to the future of the island would simply eliminate many of the proclaimed infrastructure construction and expansion needs. To my mind, this equates with park resource protection.

A major assumption in the 2004 Master Plan Update and in the Bleakly Advisory Group impact analysis was that the economy, including financial markets, housing markets, tourism markets, and other key areas that determine demand for Jekyll Island amenities, will be stable and growing as in the past. The Bleakly Advisory Group analysis and Master Plan assumptions are obviously way off the mark. During the time Bleakly's analysis was being done, there had been a deep recession and housing market bust that was not properly taken into account.

3. The "Density" of the Smoke Increases

Another phase of the Bleakly impact analysis was stated as "an examination of the context for understanding the impact of development on visitor experiences." Making this statement seemed to me as close to examining visitor experiences as either the Bleakly Advisory Group or the Authority ever came. The parks and recreation professional approaches to measuring and monitoring visitor experiences did not enter this analysis. A respected reference, among the many that exist, could have been Glaspell, et al (2003). And of note, the Bleakly Advisory Group analysis results were reported to the Jekyll Island Authority nearly two months *after* signing the development contract.

Apparently, the context for understanding visitor experiences is to measure how much the density of visitors and housing will increase as a result of commercial development. In examining this phase of the Bleakly analysis,

I used the same professional standards one would expect to
use in reviewing a paper or report written for a professional
outlet. An example of such an outlet is the *Journal of Park
and Recreation Administration* (JPRA). The development
pursued by the Jekyll Island Authority and Linger Longer
will change in perpetuity the character of Jekyll Island State
Park. Thus, holding the Bleakly Advisory Group impact
analysis to the same professional standards as other park and
recreation administration research reports seems appropriate.
(For the record, to my knowledge no park and recreation
professionals were ever asked by the Jekyll Island Authority
to review the Bleakly Advisory Group analyses. Also for the
record, had I had the opportunity, I would have concluded
that for the JPRA this work should be rejected. It does not
meet professional park standards.)

The primary approach used for this phase of the Bleakly
Advisory Group analysis was to compare development and
population densities in Jekyll Island State Park, before and
after commercial development, with density on other east
coast islands. The first flaw in the analysis was that it did not
consider visitor experiences or the park's cultural or natural
resources. The second flaw was that the island area in acres
used in the Bleakly calculations were more than double
recent LIDAR-based estimates (state-of-the-art and from the
University of Georgia) of the actual state park's land area.
The Bleakly Advisory Group analysis compared the density
of other east coast islands with development and population

densities before and after Jekyll Island development, therefore it was crucial to carefully identify and use the correct island area estimate. Instead, the visitor and housing densities reported were seriously understated to be only about one-half of the actual densities. The island area used included huge expanses of marsh and the six-mile long causeway, which are not part of the island's land area.

As an example of how the inflated total island area greatly understated development density on Jekyll Island, the number of commercial lodging units currently on the island (1,208) was compared with Captiva/Sanibel Island, an island that is heavily developed. Total number of commercial lodging units on Jekyll Island after development in the year 2023 is projected at 3,370. This is sixty-five percent greater than the much larger Captiva/Sanibel. After adjusting Jekyll Island to its correct land area, a little over 4,000 acres as opposed to 9,232 acres as used in the Bleakly Advisory Group analysis, the island's density in 2009 is greater than Captiva/Sanibel at 0.3 units per acre. Comparing units per acre of resident housing between Captiva/Sanibel Island and Jekyll Island State Park shows that Jekyll Island, by 2023, would be substantially above Captiva/Sanibel. In fact, the density of Jekyll Island in 2023 *would exceed development of any other coastal island* selected by the Bleakly Advisory Group and the Jekyll Island Authority as comparisons. This includes exceeding Pawley's and Santa Rosa Islands. The projected density for Jekyll Island would be nearly four times the density of St. Simons Island. The Bureau of Census definition for an urban area is 500 or more persons per square mile. Population density projected for Jekyll Island by 2023, after development, would be more than twice the Bureau of Census definition of an urban area.

The figure on page 201 shows the number of persons staying overnight per square mile for ten coastal islands, including Jekyll Island in 2008 and in 2023. Persons per square mile on Jekyll Island State Park was reported by the Bleakly Advisory Group as 254 in 2008 and at 546 for 2023. After correcting the land area within these computations from the incorrect 9,232 to the more correct area of 4,152 acres, the corrected population density for Jekyll Island in 2008 is computed at 565. The corrected forecast population density for Jekyll in 2023 is 1,213. The density reported by Bleakly Advisory Group for 2023 was 546, less than one-half the correct calculation.

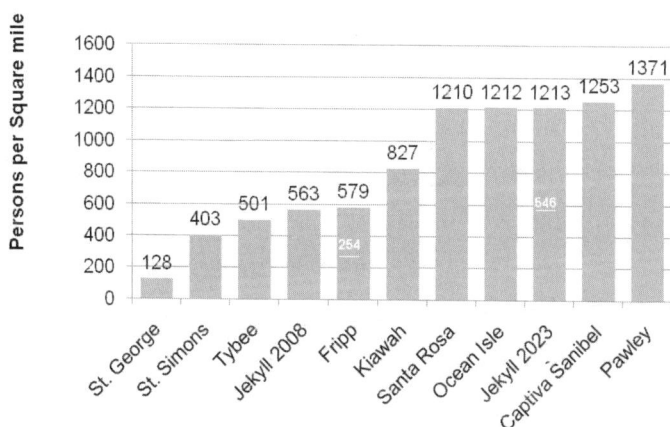

Compared Islands

Comparison of peak overnight population per square mile occupying dwelling units and commercial lodging for ten southeastern coastal islands, including Jekyll Island State Park in 2008 and in 2023, after commercial development. All figures are for 2008 except the bar marked "Jekyll 2023."

4. What Mirror Image Can We See in Private Profiting from Sales of Oceanfront Timeshares and Condominiums?

Most of the privately-owned portions of the coasts of the United States are heavily developed. At this time, Jekyll Island is among those not heavily developed. However, as indicated earlier, in December of 2008, the Jekyll Island State Park Authority signed a long-term, exclusive contract with a commercial private development corporation. That corporation is Linger Longer Communities based in Greensboro, Georgia.

When commercial development is planned for private oceanfront land, the private owner will surely insist on fair market compensation for the rights to develop and sell properties on his or her land. This would include rents and profit sharing. Currently prime, commercially-zoned ocean-front land (including Jekyll Island) is worth at least $3 million per acre. Properties worth $3 million or more per acre obviously benefit from good location with highly desirable amenities (such as ocean views, ocean frontage and beach access).

Low development, high-amenity properties such as Jekyll Island are worth far more than other properties. This added worth is referred to in real estate economics as a price premium. The higher the price premium on land to be used commercially, the higher should be the financial returns to the owners. In the instance of the Linger Longer-Jekyll Island Authority development contract, however, it seems the price premium of the highly desirable publicly-owned Jekyll Island oceanfront was not fully assessed.

To properly address the question of what "fair returns" should mean for Jekyll Island, published economics and real estate appraisal journal research literature were consulted. The objective for consulting this research was to identify the credible range of applicable price and land value premiums (percentage increases in market value) associated with properties having a view of and/or being located on oceanfront.

The abundant cache of research I reviewed showed that properties rich with natural amenities are worth substantially more. This includes properties such as condominiums and single family housing with views and access to forests, water, wildlife, clean air, oceans and many other natural amenities. Examples of this research include Crompton (2007) who reported that the positive impact of views and park access adds at least twenty percent (this is the sales price premium) onto the values of residential properties. Filippova (2009) looked at over 53,000 residential sales transactions and surmised that price premium added was fifty-four percent for ocean views in posh communities. A study by Seiler, Bond and Seiler (2001) showed that having an ocean-like view increased home value by approximately fifty-six percent, while having a home on the shoreline of Lake Erie increased home prices 93.3 percent. Benson et al. (1998) studied ocean frontage properties and found that frontage added 147 percent to the price of residential property. Major, Christopher, and Luscht (2004) looked at distance to oceanfront and revealed that distance was inversely related to the price premium and that the oceanfront price premium was 156 percent. Thus, ocean and other waterfront locations with water views add roughly fifty-five to over 150 percent to residential property sales values.

I applied the oceanfront price premiums to the Jekyll

Island condominium development plans to see what profit-sharing would be appropriate between citizen-owners and Linger Longer. Sales of the timeshares and condominiums on Jekyll Island State Park are predicted to produce gross sales revenues of approximately $163 million (Bleakly Advisory Group 2009b). Total development investment cost for the planned condominiums is estimated at $37.5 million. Advertising and promotion (marketing) costs for selling the condominiums and timeshares was estimated using research from Texas A&M's Real Estate Center and the National Association of Realtors (NAR). NAR's estimated median marketing costs are about 8.2 percent of gross revenues. Thus, efficient marketing of the planned timeshares on the identified prime oceanfront Jekyll Island park property should not be more than $13.4 million.

A reasonable estimate of profit yield on the Linger Longer condominium and timeshare sales, therefore, would be roughly $112.1 million ($163M − ($37.5M + $13.4M) = $112.1M) (see figure on page 205). The contracted financial arrangement signed by the Jekyll Island Authority with Linger Longer requires a payment total to the Authority over the life of the project of just $1.63 million. This is about one percent of gross revenues and about 1.4 percent of profits beyond development and marketing costs. While Linger Longer is also required to pay rental on an annual ground lease for the condominium and timeshare site, this payment does not affect profits from the sale of these residences because lease payments and after-sale site rental and maintenance costs for the timeshares and condominiums will be paid by the buyers.

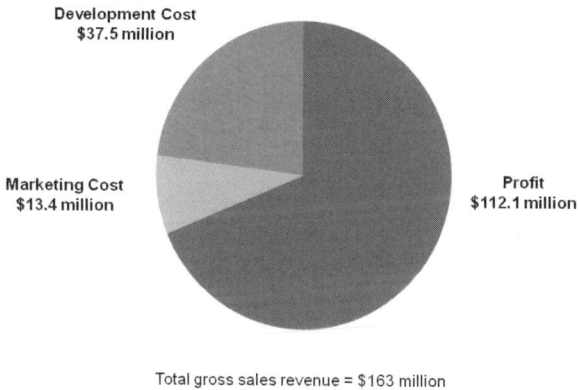

Total gross sales revenue = $163 million

Projected total revenues, costs, and profit from the development and sales of timeshares and condominiums on Jekyll Island.

Rental is addressed in the next section of this chapter.

A return of just 1.4 percent of timeshare profits does not adequately reflect the value of the citizen-owned, oceanfront property relative to the value of the condominiums and timeshares to be built. The published research summarized above indicated that oceanfront land premiums range from about eighty-two percent (The Land Policy Institute at Michigan State University 2003) to 156 percent (Major, Christopher, and Luscht 2004). Taking a mid-point between the lower and upper values of this range shows that the condominiums to be developed and sold by Linger Longer will be worth around 119 percent more than the same condominiums located elsewhere, not on oceanfront land. We can reasonably assume that well designed and constructed condominiums would normally sell for about $400,000, if not on oceanfront land. On oceanfront with the oceanfront price premium added, these same condominiums would sell for around $876,000.

Thus, I calculated that the condominium units of the planned quality, including landscaping and other amenities, will account for roughly forty-six percent of the total market value of the oceanfront condominiums and timeshares, while the citizen-owned oceanfront site where these residences are to be developed will contribute roughly fifty-four percent of market value. It appears then, that a more equitable profit sharing arrangement would be to distribute forty-six percent of profits to the commercial condominium-timeshare developer and fifty-four percent to the public park owner. A forty-six percent share of the $112 million in profits is approximately $52 million, which seems a generous return to a private investor who does not own the land to be developed. This is more than a 100-percent profit ($52 million profit beyond the $50.9 million cost = 102% return above cost). A fifty-four percent return share of the estimated $112.1 million in profits to the citizen-owners, for use in improving and protecting Jekyll Island State Park, would be approximately $60 million. Anything less than $60 million would seriously undervalue the commercially zoned state park oceanfront location, which is not only oceanfront, but is also surrounded by highly desirable state park land. Thus, if the agreed-to profit shares (which are ninety-nine percent to the private developer and one percent to the state park) are looked at in the mirror, one can see only a faint, ghostly image of what the citizens' share should be.

5. Not Only Fair Profit Sharing, but Also Fair Rent for Use of the State Park Land

What then does one see as a mirror image when rent being charged to the developer is reflected? Do we see clearly that full rent is being paid to citizen-owners for development and profiting rights to Jekyll Island State Park? In addition to profit-sharing from sales of timeshares and condominium units, a fair market rent should be paid for the right to occupy the development site, which will essentially prohibit recreational use by Jekyll Island visitors in perpetuity. Given that commercially zoned, oceanfront land, with ocean view, wide beaches, and direct access is currently selling for at least $3 million per acre, one could question whether the ground lease of approximately $400,000 annually given to Linger Longer is an appropriate rental. The analysis performed by the Bleakly Advisory Group reported that the per-acre value of this site is just under $800,000 per acre, only twenty-seven percent of the true, very reasonable per-acre market value (see figure on page 208). In addition, new infrastructure to the timeshare and condominium site is to be

provided through public financing by the state and the
Authority, which adds to the profitability of the project for
the developer.

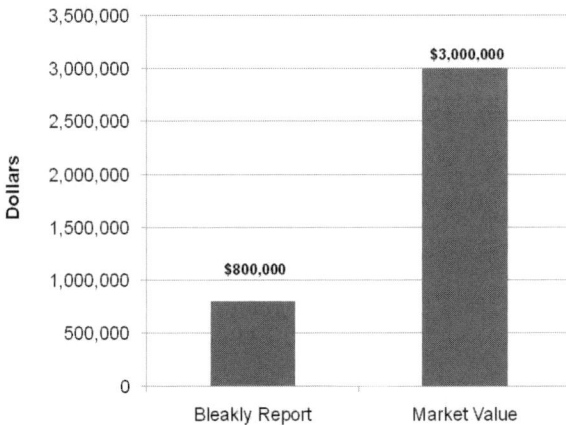

*Value of development site in dollars per acre — Bleakly and true
market values.*

In a free market economy, owners of residential and
commercial development would have to pay fair market rent
for the right to occupy oceanfront land. From economics we
know that rent is the product of the market value of land
multiplied by its capitalization rate. Oceanfront, commercially
developable land can easily carry a seven-to-nine percent
capitalization rate. At $3 million per acre, the 5.5 acres on
which the time-shares are to be developed is worth a total of
$16.5 million. At a seven percent capitalization rate, a fair
market-based rental should be $16.5 million x 0.07 = $1.155
million annually. At a nine percent capitalization rate, a fair

market-based rental should be $16.5 million x 0.09 = $1.485 million annually. Even if the fair market capitalization rate were as low as five percent, the rental would be $16.5 million x 0.05 = $825,000, still twice the ground lease negotiated by the Authority. Ground lease rent and all other costs of the timeshares will be borne by the buyers after sale and thus will not affect the sale profits. A $400,000 ground lease rental annually (a rental fee that would be waived during the two-year construction period) is less than thirty percent of the rent that should paid to the owners of this land, the people of Georgia.

Closing Observations

Parks and recreation has been my profession and research area for many years. It is my belief that my experience and publication record qualify me to comment on the decision process employed by the Jekyll Island Authority, and on the contract terms signed with Linger Longer Communities. Jekyll Island is a state park entrusted to be managed for citizens, for visitors (and not for development of private housing), and for the park resources in perpetuity. In my view, there has been too much smoke to be able to see clearly where this island's future lies. But from all appearances, and unless something changes, it seems that future will be revenue and profit driven.

Just like my work, the Bleakly Advisory Group's reports and analyses should be subjected to rigorous peer review. Such

peer review seems especially needed in light of the fact that
Jekyll Island is a state park, not private property. Accounting
only for revenue, development, and population densities as
criteria for managing a public property is inappropriate and
inconsistent with widely known and professionally endorsed
park and public land planning standards. This approach also is
not consistent with state of Georgia planning principles, with
the Georgia Statewide Comprehensive Outdoor Recreation
Plan, or with the Department of Natural Resources and Georgia
State Park strategic plans.

It seems that only one option has been considered for the
future of this jewel of a state park. That option is commercial
development that moves the island toward being *one of the
most developed barrier islands on the Southeast coast*, one
whose peak seasonal population per square mile would be more
than twice the Bureau of Census definition of an urban area.

Valid, reliable, and documented estimates of visitation,
revenue needs, and development impacts are crucial to
decisions about the future of any publicly owned area. But
these should not be the only, or even the primary bases for
park management decisions. At Jekyll Island, the use of
inconsistent traffic flow monitoring data resulted in
questionable visitation estimates and decisions to commercially
develop a state park. The decision to commercially develop
led to projections of costs and revenues that to me seem
unnecessary. Signing a long-term development contract
without adequate analyses of market trends (tourism,

financing, etc.) puts the future of Jekyll Island State Park at risk. Using estimates of development and population densities that seemed to seriously understate the impact of park development fails to take account of desires of park visitors. First and foremost, Jekyll Island is a state park and it should be managed as such. In my opinion, it should not be managed to maximize revenues and profits.

Chapter 11
Contract Epilogue

On December 8, 2009, the contract between the Jekyll Island Authority and Linger Longer Communities was suspended. According to the *Atlanta Journal Constitution*, the Authority announced that it had ended the deal, and the Web site *Atlanta Unfiltered* reported that although Linger Longer had pulled out, both parties agreed to suspend the agreement. This was seen as a victory for Georgia citizens who oppose extensive development, but the Jekyll Island Authority expressed a commitment to quickly move forward with the planned development anyway. This time, the Authority said it would contract each component separately, such as the convention center, the retail center, and the timeshares and condominiums. According to Dan Chapman, writing on December 9, 2009 in the *Atlanta Journal Constitution*:

> Jekyll Island State Park's upscale redevelopment plans hit the skids Tuesday when the main developer pulled out of the project.

Opponents of the plan who prefer slower growth cheered the decision by Linger Longer Communities, the politically influential company that owns Reynolds Plantation ninety minutes east of Atlanta, to quit the $170 million hotel-condo-retail development. They called it a victory for budget-conscious, beach-loving Georgians, many of whom got a first whiff of salt air along Jekyll's shores.

Disappointed Jekyll Island officials, along with Governor Sonny Perdue who championed a revitalized Jekyll five years ago, vowed that reconstruction of the state-owned barrier island near Brunswick will continue. A new retail district, convention center and beachfront park remain on the books. (2009b)

The Jekyll Island Authority issued a press release noting that, in the now revised plan for development, "the amount of private-sector investment is expected to be at least if not more than the $120 million. Each private-sector component — two hotels, 30,000 square feet of retail with condominium lofts and vacation ownership units — will represent a unique hospitality investment opportunity." Thus, it appears that the Jekyll Island Authority is still not listening to the voice of the citizen-owners of Jekyll Island State Park.

IPJI Co-director David Egan, in reviewing the change in the Authority's plans, wrote in an email on December 29, 2009 that the bottom line remains — the citizens of Georgia are losing public space in the town center project. He said:

> This loss is even more important when considering
> that the public space to be lost currently serves as
> Jekyll's most widely used beachfront parking area.
> With Georgia's coastal population growing annually
> at a double digit rate, and with Jekyll being Georgia's
> only barrier island state park, one would think that
> the Jekyll Island Authority board would realize that
> public demand for access to Jekyll's most tide-
> friendly beach will increase. Yet, this board insists
> that displacing beachside public facilities with
> privately owned time-shares is what Jekyll needs in
> order to be 'revitalized.'

Egan also pointed out that the convention center should be renovated, rather than torn down and rebuilt as the Jekyll Island Authority plans to do. In an IPJI survey of seventy-five Jekyll Island convention groups, Egan noted that eighty-five percent of conventioneers responding to the survey found the convention center adequate, and almost sixty percent reported it was excellent or above average when compared with other convention centers. Tearing down and rebuilding this center, therefore, is a waste of dollars and resources. Renovation appears to be the most reasonable option for the convention center. Unfortunately, the Jekyll Island Authority seems to have already made its decision, and it is not clear why it decided that a new convention center is needed. Did the Jekyll Island Authority even consider renovation?

In a December 15, 2009 opinion editorial for the *Savannah Morning News*, Egan also noted that the breakdown of the Linger Longer deal provides "a window of opportunity for the Authority's board to try to accomplish this task in harmony with public opinion instead of in opposition to it, as has too often been the case over the past two years." Egan claimed that the involvement of the public, while taking additional time up front, will save the Jekyll Island Authority time and dollars in the long run. Any plan developed with the intimate involvement of citizens, he said, would be supported by the public, and would avoid many of the pitfalls of the earlier plans.

Citizen response, once again, left no doubt as to what average Georgians thought about the suspension of the contract. Online comments in response to an *Athens Banner-Herald* article on the contract suspension, include this thought from "ThreeDollarBill:"

Amen. I don't understand what seems like a primordial drive to develop the island. Those 1.49 million people seem to enjoy [the island as it is]. It's also not as if it's a facility like the Georgia World Congress Center that has to be used. The island will do just fine, just sitting there. This is a classic case of a group with a little power looking for something to justify their existence. I guess inquiring minds want to know [that] if a politically-wired developer like Linger Longer can't find financing, where are second tier developers going to find financing?

From "dahreese:"

In spite of thousands of protests and inputs from thousands of Georgians and people outside of Georgia who visit the island because of its naturalness…, what the [Authority] intends to do is to continue to ram its unnecessary projects down the throats of the Georgia people, wanted or not. The [Authority] is made up of business/political people with a "money mentality" who see Jekyll Island as nothing but another cash cow and who just can't understand why someone, anyone, would want to walk over an undeveloped beach. Hopefully those of you who care to keep the island as natural as possible and not make it into another Hilton Head or Disneyland, will contact [the Authority] and let them know how you feel.

Although Linger Longer Communities may be out of the picture, the Jekyll Island Authority appeared, in January 2010, to be committed to moving ahead, again without following best practices in outdoor recreation planning. These best practices were outlined in Chapter 3. I remember them by the acronym VEE-SIPPI (Visitor Experiences, Environment, Science, Involvement, Park Purpose, and Interdisciplinary). In an opinion editorial in the *Savannah Morning* News on December 19, 2009, Jekyll Island Authority Chairman Bob Krueger provided, in his words, an "insider's perspective" of what will happen on Jekyll Island after the failed Linger Longer contract. Using the metaphor of a football game, Krueger vowed that the Authority would "tighten our chin straps and work towards the goal" of continued development. Then, following up with a revealing remark, Krueger said, "Critics abound, and I liken them to armchair quarterbacks yelling at the television suggesting they could make better play calls than the professionals on the field. They yell and scream, then ask to pass the chips." I find it arrogant that Krueger, who should be working *for* the people of Georgia, would call those expressing their legitimate opinions "armchair quarterbacks." Further, Krueger's team "on the field" is filled with realtors, bankers, and businessmen, not professionals in the field of outdoor recreation, public land planning, and public service. Krueger's comments are an insult to professionals in the field of outdoor recreation who operate using professional guidelines, standards, and best practices, and who welcome the participation of the public.

In an article published in the December 30, 2009 *Atlanta Journal-Constitution*, Dan Chapman reported that "the board that runs the state park is already lining up new developers who might instead build the hotels, condos, and shops once planned for the southeast Georgia barrier island." It appears that the Authority does not plan to slow down and ask the public what it would like to see on Jekyll Island State Park.

By the time this book is published, more will be known about the Authority's intentions. Has it continued on the same road, excluding the public from its deliberations and decisions; or has it embraced best practices in outdoor recreation planning?

A Good Example for the Jekyll Island Authority

On December 17, 2009, the U.S. Forest Service issued a press release (Release No. 0620.09) announcing a Notice of Intent (NOI) to develop a new process for national forest planning. This is the kind of announcement I believe the citizens of Georgia would welcome regarding Jekyll Island State Park. As you read below, imagine these words coming from the Jekyll Island Authority.

The Forest Service is seeking public involvement in developing a new direction for local land managers. A 60-day comment period on the Notice of Intent (NOI) will begin upon publication in the Federal Register on Friday, December 18, 2009. Comments will be used to shape the focus of the collaborative dialogue and creation of a proposed [planning process].

To begin the conversation, the Forest Service has included in the NOI a set of potential principles that could guide development of a new planning [process]. The potential principles include an emphasis on restoration, conservation, and the improved resilience of ecosystems; watershed health; climate change response; species diversity and wildlife habitat; sustainable National Forest System lands; proactive collaboration; and working across landscapes.

The Forest Service will use state-of-the-art new media tools in conjunction with face-to-face interaction to facilitate wide public participation throughout the nation. Please visit www.fs.usda.gov/planningrule to participate in our web-based planning rule blog, and to learn more.

Note that the Forest Service is inviting the public to help them develop the collaborative process of planning, and is not simply asking for input into a predetermined process. This is the kind of collaborative thinking and approach that would well serve Jekyll Island State Park, the Jekyll Island Authority, and Jekyll's citizen-owners. In a January 10, 2010 email to me from Executive Director Jones Hooks regarding the planning process used by the Authority, Mr. Hooks told me, "While Jekyll Island is a state-owned facility, we do not operate as part of the State Park System of Georgia — nor under the policies of the National Park Service." Mr. Hooks further noted that, "…while the Initiative to Protect Jekyll Island may have ten thousand voices from around the country, please remember there are over seven million Georgians that have ownership in Jekyll Island." Of those ten thousand voices, over seven thousand are Georgia citizens. I hope Mr. Hooks was not discounting those seven thousand voices. I was, however, glad to hear that Mr. Hooks understands that the citizens of Georgia are the owners of Jekyll Island. Now, let's hope that the owners of Jekyll Island get to have a say in the island's future.

Only time will tell if the Jekyll Island Authority will embrace an open, transparent, and citizen-driven planning process. By the time you are reading these words, the answer may well be known. To discover what is happening now, visit the IPJI Web site at www.savejekyllisland.org.

Chapter 12
Grassroots Action Makes a Difference

Georgia Sierra Club — The Initiative to Protect Jekyll Island provided an outstanding example of grassroots citizen lobbying in winning this victory [the preservation of the public access area north of the convention center] over the toughest of opponents: a fabulously wealthy and influential developer, a toadying state agency, and the lobbying of former Natural Resources Commissioner Joe D. Tanner, the most formidable insider of them all. The Sierra Club was pleased to be able to work with such outstanding folks... (Sierra Club 2008)

The recent history of Jekyll Island is at the very least a story of inappropriate planning for public land, and an apparent devaluing of public participation in government. What would have happened, however, had a couple of retired transplants from the Northeast not become committed to protecting Jekyll Island?

I first met David and Mindy Egan in 2006. We met at the commercial center on Jekyll Island, all of us straddling bicycles. David and Mindy were doing what they could to get public input injected into the Jekyll Island Authority's deliberations about Jekyll's future. They had created a survey and with the cooperation of some Jekyll hotel owners and merchants, they placed these surveys around the island. A cardboard box on their front porch provided a convenient repository for the surveys, or one could mail the survey to their home. They called their effort the Initiative to Protect Jekyll Island, or IPJI.

David and Mindy had fallen in love with Jekyll Island after their first visit to the island. They decided after that first visit to downsize their lifestyle and save as much money as possible, so that they could retire to Jekyll Island. Their dream was realized in 1997 when they moved to a home on the western side of Georgia's jewel.

I asked Mindy about the beginning of the Initiative to Protect Jekyll Island. I wanted to learn about their motivation for giving up retirement and beginning new "careers" as activists. In an email on June 3, 2009, Mindy told me:

> Our recollection of why we started all of this is indignation over the way the Jekyll Island Authority was getting "input" for "revitalization," that is, relying on input meetings held on Jekyll which were attended predominately, if not exclusively, by Jekyll residents. As visitors for many years prior to becoming residents, we simply could not understand how or why the Jekyll Island Authority could be planning for the island's future without taking into account the wishes and interests of the park's visitors. We saw us,

the residents, as secondary to the process and just very, very fortunate people to be able to live in such a fantastic environment. The experience of a beach setting of such incredible natural magnitude and the affordability of the island's accommodations were beyond anything we had ever seen in all our trips scouring the east coast looking for the ideal place. And, we have always LOVED seeing visitors discover the wonders of Jekyll...most residents do...they go out of their way to tell visitors of interesting, unpublicized spots or things to do. It is awesome to see kids see the ocean and just go wild with excitement!

And the other big concern was what would happen to Jekyll's environment and the wonderful open feeling of being surrounded by nature, whether riding your bike down the beach or along the marsh, walking the golf course or touring the Historic District, where the buildings fit into rather than overtake nature.

After the Egans began to collect visitor comments, they were overwhelmed by the hundreds of impassioned pleas from visitors to protect the island. (The comments interspersed throughout this book provide a small sample of the thousands of comments they have received. More comments can be read at www.savejekyllisland.org.) The Egans were moved by the stories of childhood vacations, weddings, and family outings on Jekyll. As they received more comments, they

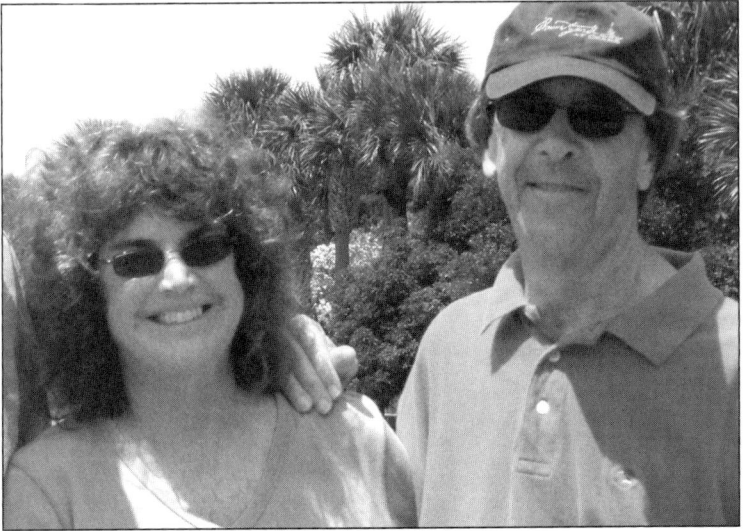

Mindy and David Egan, Co-directors, Initiative to Protect Jekyll Island.

became more determined and slowly began to realize the scale and complexity of the task ahead. They, like many grassroots organizers, had never done anything like this before. Improvements came slowly, along with volunteers. A Web site was established. A metro Atlanta chapter was established. An Athens group was established. More people volunteered. The Initiative to Protect Jekyll Island began having an impact.

The Initiative to Protect Jekyll Island has been enormously successful. With the support of other non-profit groups and a few legislators, IPJI has built an impressive track record of accomplishment.

Were it not for IPJI and registered volunteer lobbyist Dory Ingram, Senator Jeff Chapman, Representative Debbie

Buckner, House Minority Leader Dubose Porter, and lobbyists Neil Herring and Mark Woodall with the Sierra Club, the residents of Jekyll led by Frank Mirasola (and many others), the environmentally-sensitive south end of Jekyll Island would be on its way to being a commercial zone, packed with condominiums, single family estate homes, and a boutique hotel. Instead, by law it is now protected from further development.

Some of the other professionals who have worked with IPJI to protect Jekyll Island at the General Assembly are:

• David Kyler, Center for a Sustainable Coast

• Gordon Rogers (formerly Satilla Riverkeeper, now Flint Riverkeeper)

• Jill Johnson (formerly Georgia Conservancy, now with Georgia Conservation Voters)

• Glenn Dowling, Georgia Wildlife Federation

• Jason Rooks, Georgia Conservation Voters

• Pam Davidson, Jekyll Island Citizens' Association

• Art and Lisa Hurt, Atlanta Audubon Society

• Mary Lovings, Garden Club of Georgia

IPJI board member Dory Ingram established the Atlanta metro chapter of the Initiative to Protect Jekyll Island. She has worked tirelessly to keep Atlanta citizens informed and prior to 2010, coordinated IPJI's efforts to communicate with the General Assembly. Dory has also produced videos about Jekyll Island which can be viewed on the IPJI Web site or on YouTube.

Thanks to IPJI members Steve and Bonnie Newell, Jekyll Island has a modern turtle lighting ordinance. The Newells painstakingly researched Florida's model ordinances and worked with the Jekyll Island Authority to develop an ordinance that can sustain the nesting of loggerhead turtles on Jekyll. Steve collected and disseminated information about Jekyll's maritime forest, alerting citizens and the Jekyll Island Authority of its fragility and the need to protect it from development. The Newells continue to be vigilant overseers of Jekyll's precious ecological systems.

Without IPJI, citizens statewide would have had no voice in the Jekyll Island issue. The Jekyll Island Authority has seemed to ignore public comments and has not appeared to provide an appropriate and honest forum for public participation. IPJI has provided the main mechanism by which the citizen-owners of Jekyll Island have been heard regarding the development and future of their state park. IPJI has provided legislators and the Authority with hard copies of the thousands of comments received from Jekyll supporters statewide, nationwide, and in fact, worldwide.

IPJI has provided the only evidence we have of the multiple values the citizen-owners of Jekyll place on the island. The IPJI Web site (www.savejekyllisland.org) is a wealth of information about Jekyll Island and the rush to development. The Web site also contains photo galleries and other interesting information about Jekyll Island.

IPJI questioned the calculations done of the island's acreage, resulting in the Jekyll Island Authority's admittance that they have fifty percent fewer acres to develop than they previously claimed.

IPJI has been a watchdog of the studies done by the Bleakly Advisory Group to support the Authority's activities and decisions. This has resulted in some instances of back-pedaling by the Jekyll Island Authority. For example, IPJI continued to question the visitation figures presented by the Authority, with an eventual change in the percentage decline admitted by the Authority from fifty percent to twenty percent.

David and Mindy have been at the center of a storm of activity to protect Jekyll Island. They and IPJI, which has over 10,000 members nationwide, have won three prestigious statewide awards. In March 2008, they won the *Atlanta Journal Constitution*'s Heroes of Open Government Award. In December 2008, they were the recipients of the first annual Nick Williams Award, given by the Center for a Sustainable Coast. In April 2009, David and Mindy were honored with the Democracy Award from Georgia Common Cause.

When I asked David and Mindy what this section should include, they asked me to emphasize that grassroots action makes a difference. Rather than focus on their own accomplishments, they hope that citizens who love Jekyll Island will join IPJI (membership is free) and continue to write letters to their legislators and to newspaper editors, check the IPJI Web site regularly, and get involved in the struggle to protect Jekyll Island. See chapter 14 for a list of things you can do to help protect Jekyll Island.

In honor of David and Mindy, and of all the people who give (up) so much for what they believe and love, I hope that you will go to chapter 14 and contribute what you can to the protection of Jekyll Island. In the signature line of their email address, David and Mindy have included what I know for them is a great inspiration. It is the famous quote from Margaret Mead:

"Never doubt that a small group of thoughtful, committed citizens can change the world; indeed, it is the only thing that ever has."

Chapter 13
Remembering Jekyll Island State Park

Remember Jekyll Island is a tale of two tragedies. The first tragedy is the apparent discounting and devaluing of Georgia citizens by the Jekyll Island Authority and the Georgia General Assembly. The second tragedy is the degradation and possible loss of a treasured state park experience for Georgia's citizens and other Jekyll Island visitors.

Jekyll Island State Park's recent history appears to me to be a disturbing example of how money, power, and influence can run roughshod over average citizens. The way this has occurred makes it appear to be an ill-conceived attempt to exploit public land for private gain. Surprising relationships between the Jekyll Island Authority, the Jekyll Island Authority Legislative Oversight Committee, and a principal of Linger Longer Communities only cast additional shadows. These relationships have seemed to enable public officials to devalue with impunity public preferences and ignore the best professional practices in outdoor recreation and state park planning. We may never know the full story behind this plan to develop Jekyll Island.

We do know, however, that Jekyll Island State Park has thousands of citizen-supporters, people who not only do not want all of the development being planned, but who have spoken out against it. These are average citizens with busy lives, who have taken time to speak. It is nothing less than tragic for our state that their voices have too often been discounted. The public's voice, after all, should be the foundation of our state's actions.

Jekyll Island's visitors and citizen-owners should be the driving force behind its future.

With no way to elect a representative Jekyll Island Authority board, we are left with the hope that Georgia's next governor will hold more dearly to democratic values that encourage and respect public will. Whoever our next governor will be, he or she must understand that public exclusion from and elitism in state government cannot be tolerated. The makeup of the Jekyll Island Authority board must be changed to better represent the population of Georgia, and to bring in professionals familiar with best practices in public land, state park, and outdoor recreation planning and management. A set of qualifications should be developed for, or at least a series of training workshops should be required of, this board charged with making decisions about Georgia's jewel. We must make that clear, in spite of our busy lives.

Remember Jekyll Island began with Gifford Pinchot's observation that the best public policies are those that "provide the greatest good [for] the greatest number in the long run." It is appropriate to conclude with another thought from Pinchot (1910):

> I stand for the [Teddy] Roosevelt policies because they set the common good of all of us above the private gain of some of us; because they recognize the livelihood of the small man as more important to the nation than the profit of the big man; because they oppose all useless waste at present at the cost of robbing the future;...because they insist upon equality of opportunity and denounce monopoly and special privilege; because, discarding false issues, they deal directly with the vital questions that really make a difference with the welfare of us all; and,

most of all, **because in them the plain American always and everywhere holds the first place**. And I propose to stand for them while I have the strength to stand for anything. (Ch. II, n.p., emphasis mine)

The second tragic tale of this book is how Jekyll's visitors may be robbed of their beloved state park experience. Throughout *Remember Jekyll Island*, I have tried to convey how the people of Georgia have expressed their love for Jekyll Island. All public land is important, and Jekyll Island provides one of the most unique island state park experiences nationwide. It is the only easily accessible public land in Georgia where families can experience a natural barrier island with uncrowded beaches. Jekyll is a place where children can safely ride their bicycles without supervision, crowds, or traffic. On Jekyll Island, children discover the joy and magic of playing outdoors while learning about our precious coastal resources. Most importantly, they can escape the pressure of our consumer-dominated culture. Jekyll is a place to experience much-desired and needed "island time." On Jekyll Island, we can all reconnect to the natural world and each other, and escape for a while the hectic pace of our times.

The future signposts for Jekyll Island (Appendix 1) point to an increasingly expansive, developed, and privatized Jekyll Island beyond even current development plans. It breaks my heart for so many reasons. Let's not let it happen.

Finally, I hope this book is a wake-up call for everyone who values the opportunity to walk along a public beach, hike in a public forest, picnic in a public park, or canoe on a public waterway. Our nation's public lands are precious, they belong to us. They *are* America the Beautiful. We must not let them go.

On Jekyll Island, children have an opportunity to experience nature and escape the demands of their daily lives.

Chapter 14
What You Can Do

D. Canton, GA — I absolutely love Jekyll Island and I will do anything I can to save it!

I began working with the grassroots effort to protect Jekyll Island in the spring of 2006. I currently chair the Initiative to Protect Jekyll Island's board of directors. (Note, however, that I wrote *Remember Jekyll Island* independently of any organization.) We have had many successes in the last three-plus years. Without grassroots action and the Initiative to Protect Jekyll Island, the environmentally critical south end of Jekyll would likely be razed by now, with trophy homes and elite hotels on the schedule. Instead, the south end is protected for now from further development. The popular public beach access area north of the convention center may well have been the site of a large town center, including over 400 condominiums, timeshares, and a high-end hotel. Grassroots action and the Shore Protection Act changed all that. The Jekyll Island Authority could be proceeding on the false assumption that it has 108 acres to develop, not fifty-five (or less, perhaps none). Clearly, citizen action has made a difference.

Have we been totally successful? No, but in the face of power, money, and influence, our gains are a cause for celebration. I do not plan to give up. Public land is too important to me (and you!). Our collective love for Jekyll Island is too great to allow it to be turned over to the private sector without a fight.

You may be asking yourself, "Can I really make a difference?" The answer is YES! The successes of the Initiative to Protect Jekyll Island prove that this is so. Suggested actions are listed below. Some may be done just once; others might be done weekly or monthly. You may think of some new ones. Jekyll Island needs everyone's talents and contributions, so if you are inclined, please join the effort to protect Jekyll Island. Look around you for other public lands that might need your help. Citizen-owned public lands are part of our great American legacy. It is up to each of us to pass that legacy to our children and grandchildren.

By the time you read this, the situation on Jekyll Island will have undoubtedly changed, as the book publishing process requires at least four to five intervening months between writing and publication. In late 2009, the Jekyll Island Authority indicated it plans to continue extensive development of the island. To be sure, Jekyll Island needs your help today to minimize expansive development, ensure appropriate park improvements, and prevent the spread of private timeshares, condominiums, and golf course villas across its landscape. A visit to www.savejekyllisland.org

will give you the most recent information. Please consider the following "to do lists" as a guide to action.

Jekyll Island "To Do Lists"

Things you can do just once:

- ☐ Go to www.savejekyllisland.org and join IPJI. It's free!

- ☐ Go to www.savejekyllisland.org and sign IPJI's affordability petition.

- ☐ Go to www.savejekyllisland.org and order a free bumper sticker. Then put it on your car or tape it to the inside of the rear windshield. (Don't block your view!) While you are at it, order one for your spouse, your friends, at least one other person who will use it.

- ☐ Visit http://www.youtube.com/watch?v=KYEU fSbCdP4 and watch the video on the density study. Send the link to your friends.

- ☐ Contact the *Atlanta Journal Constitution* and ask the editors to continue covering Jekyll Island. Thank them for the coverage they have already provided. You can reach them at http://www.ajc. com/ and use the comment form at the bottom of the home page.

☐ Send photos you have taken on Jekyll Island,
   with captions and permission to use them, to
   degan@igc.org.

☐ Thank Senator Jeff Chapman for his willingness
   to listen to the people of Georgia and risk his
   political career to do what is right. You can email
   him at jeff@jeffchapman.us.

☐ Write a letter to the Brunswick-Golden Isles
   Chamber of Commerce stating that you believe
   that a properly managed state park will do more
   to support jobs in Brunswick and Glynn County
   over the long term than short-term construction
   of timeshares and condominiums on the island.
   The Chamber's contact information: 4 Glynn
   Avenue, Brunswick, Georgia 31520, 912-265-0620,
   FAX: 912-265-0629. If you have been a Jekyll
   Island visitor, let them know.

☐ Contact Georgia's governor and tell him how
   you feel about the handling of the future of Jekyll
   Island State Park. Ask him to remove the current
   Jekyll Island Authority board and appoint a new
   board, one that is professionally-trained in state
   park affairs, responsive, and accountable to the
   citizen-owners of Jekyll Island. Demand transparency
   in the management of Jekyll Island. While
   Governor Perdue is in office (in 2010), the Web

site form to use is: http://www.capwiz.com/
politicsol/mail/?id=2582&type=GV&state=GA
or search on the internet for "Governor
Perdue."

☐ When you finish this book, pass it along to
someone who is interested in Jekyll Island
State Park or in public lands. Better yet, buy a
few copies for your friends! All proceeds go to
the effort to protect Jekyll Island. (This book
may be purchased in hardcopy, or downloaded
for a reduced price as a pdf or e-book, from
www.rememberjekyllisland.com.)

☐ Contact your state senator and representative and
tell them how you feel about Jekyll Island. Ask
for their position on the effort to further develop
the island. You can find your representatives by
visiting http://www.votesmart.org/.

☐ Contact Jekyll Island Authority Executive
Director Jones Hooks and tell him how you feel
about the way the Authority has handled the
so-called "revitalization." His contact information
is 100 James Road, Jekyll Island, GA 31527,
912-635-2236, email jhooks@jekyllisland.com.

☐ Put your talents to good use! Volunteer to become
an active member of the Initiative to Protect Jekyll
Island. You may contact Co-Directors David and

Mindy Egan at degan@igc.org.

Things you can do once a week:

Copy this list and put it on your schedule for Sunday or Monday (or any other day!).

- ☐ Visit www.savejekyllisland.org to see the latest development and get information about what you can do. Send the link to one other person.

- ☐ Tell one other person about Jekyll Island.

Things you can do once a month:

- ☐ Go to www.savejekyllisland.org and donate what you can afford. IPJI operates entirely through the donations of members and supportive citizens.

- ☐ Visit a classroom, a Boy Scout or Girl Scout troop, or other youth group and tell young people what you have learned in this book about public land, public participation, and/or Jekyll Island. Visit www.savejekyllisland.org to download a student Powerpoint® presentation about Jekyll Island. Go to the "Resource Center" from the home page and scroll down to "Power Point Presentation for Teachers." You do not have to be a teacher to do this.

- ☐ Write to the editor of your local newspaper (online or hard copy) and other local publications and keep your community updated about Jekyll Island.

Things you can do as needed:

☐ Respond to the Initiative to Protect Jekyll Island's calls for action. (Tell IPJI you want to be placed on the group's "activist" list.) Forward the call to action to others who may be interested.

☐ Post responses to newspaper articles, blogs, or other information about Jekyll Island.

☐ Above all, keep working for Jekyll Island and public land!

Chapter 15
Resources

Organizations

Initiative to Protect Jekyll Island: www.savejekyllisland.org
Center for a Sustainable Coast (Georgia):
www.sustainablecoast.org
Common Cause (Georgia): http://www.commoncause.org/
Click on States, then click on Georgia
Trust for Public Land: http://www.tpl.org/
National Public Lands Day: http://www.publiclandsday.org/

Government
Jekyll Island Legislative Oversight Committee
Please note: If you wish to contact a member of the Oversight
Committee, a fax may be the best option. A telephone call or
postal mail is more effective than an e-mail message.

Senate Members:

Senator Chip Pearson (R)
321-B State Capitol
Atlanta, GA 30334
Chip.pearson@senate.ga.gov
404-656-9221 (Atlanta office)
678-341-6203 (district office)
Fax: 404-657-3248 (Capitol); 770-844-5821 (district)

Senator Ross Tolleson (R)
121-C State Capitol
Atlanta, GA 30334
Ross.tolleson@senate.ga.gov
478-988-1206 (office); 478-987-0325 (home)
Fax: 404-651-6767

Senator Tommie Williams (R)
236 State Capitol
Atlanta, GA 30334
Tommie@tommiewilliams.com
tommie.williams@senate.ga.gov
912-526-7444
Fax: 404-463-5220 (Capitol)

House Members:

Rep. Terry Barnard (R)
401 State Capitol
Atlanta, GA 30334
terry.barnard@house.ga.gov
912-654-1048 (home)

Rep. Jerry Keen (R)
338 State Capitol
Atlanta, GA 30334
jerry.keen@house.ga.gov
404-656-5025 (office)
Fax: 912-634-3455 (district)

Rep. Karla Drenner (D)
Suite 507 Coverdell Legislative Office Building
Atlanta, GA 30334
dren16999@aol.com
404-656-0202

The Governor:
Governor Sonny Perdue's Web-based contact form
(through 2010): http://www.capwiz.com/politicsol/
mail/?id=2582&type=GV&state=GA.

Senator Jeff Chapman, R-Brunswick: www.jeffchapman.us
District Office:
P.O. Box 3119
Brunswick, GA 31521
Email: jeff@jeffchapman.us
Cell: 912-399-8683
Fax: 404-463-2279 (Capitol)

Georgia Division of State Parks and Historic Sites
Becky Kelley, Director
Web-based contact form: http://www.gastateparks.org/net/go/
contactparks.aspx?et=8&s=0.0.1.5
2 MLK Jr. Dr. SE, Suite 1352
East Atlanta, GA 30334
404-656-2770, 1-800-864-7275

Georgia Department of Natural Resources
Chris Clark, Commissioner (and ex-officio member of the Jekyll
Island Authority)
2 MLK Jr. Dr., SE,
Suite 1252 East,
Atlanta, GA 30334
Phone: (404) 656-3500
Fax: (404) 656-0770

Jekyll Island State Park Authority

Jekyll Island State Park Authority
C. Jones Hooks, Executive Director
Robert (Bob) Krueger, Chairman
100 James Road
Jekyll Island, GA 31527
912-635-2236
jhooks@jekyllisland.com
http://www.jekyllislandauthority.org

Environment

Georgia Environmental Policy Act (Environmental Effects
Report) Checklist: http://www.usg.edu/ehs/guidelines/checklist.
pdf and Appendix 4

Completing Georgia Environmental Policy Act Evaluations:
http://www.usg.edu/ehs/guidelines/gepa.phtml

Jekyll Island Authority Beach Lighting Ordinance: http://www.
jekyllislandauthority.org/Ordinances/beach_lighting_
ordinance_2008.pdf

References

Atlanta Business Chronicle. 2008. Reynolds Plantation developer acquires N. C. golf community. *American City Business Journals, Inc.* December 31. http://atlanta.bizjournals.com/atlanta/stories/2008/12/29/daily38.html (accessed March 14, 2009).

Bagwell, Tyler E. 2001. *Jekyll Island: A state park.* Charleston, SC: Arcadia Publishing.

Benson, E. D., J. L. Hansen, A. L. Schwartz, and G. T. Smersh. 1998. Pricing residential amenities: The value of a view. *Journal of Real Estate Finance and Economics* 16, no. 1: 55-73.

Berger, Bruce. 2002. Wildness and posterity. *Land that we love: Americans talk about America's public lands.* Book published for the Olympic Arts Festival, Salt Lake 2002, n.p., http://publiclands.org/homenew.p hp?newsid=EpVyulAkypXWqLQBuL&SID=%3Chtml.

Bleakly Advisory Group. 2009a. *An analysis of the residential land lease policy on Jekyll Island, Georgia* (Draft), July 21. http://www.jekyllislandauthority.org/Jekyll_Residential_Land_Lease_Analysis_Report_7_21_09.pdf (accessed August 10, 2009).

———. 2009b. *Jekyll Island State Park Authority visitor analysis and business plan — Final report.* Atlanta GA, February. http://www.jekyllislandauthority.org/VisitationFinal0309.pdf (accessed December 28, 2009).

Burns, K. 2009. In Duncan, D. 2009. *The national parks: America's best idea.* New York: Alfred A. Knopf, p. xv.

Cabin Bluff Management. 2007. *Jekyll Island conservation plan.* http://www.jekyllislandauthority.org/jia_conservation_plan_part1.pdf (accessed March 14, 2009) and http://www.jekyllislandauthority.org/jia_conservation_plan_part2.pdf (accessed March 27, 2009).

Chapman, Dan. 2007. Jekyll's south end saved from development, *Atlanta Journal-Constitution* April 20. http://www.savejekyllisland. org/politics/ (accessed April 22, 2007).

————. 2008. Jekyll Island figures don't add up: State auditor reports that visitor figures are good. *Atlanta Journal-Constitution*, March 3. http:// www.jeffchapman.us/jekyll-renovation.html (accessed September 12, 2009).

————. 2009a. Jekyll Island Authority courting new developers. *Atlanta Journal Constitution*, December 30.

————. 2009b. Jekyll upscale redeveloper backs out of project. *Atlanta Journal Constitution*, December 9. http://www.savejekyllisland.org/ AJCDealDeadDec809.html (accessed December 20, 2009).

Chapman, Jeff. 2008a. Jekyll Island development: Con: Lopsided deal unfair to Georgians. *Atlanta Journal Constitution*, December 18. http://www. savejekyllisland.org/AJC08.html (accessed April 4, 2009).

————. 2009. Letter to the Governor and the Legislature, January 29. http://www.savejekyllisland.org/proposal.html (accessed March 15, 2009).

Chapman, Kathy. 2007. Kathy Chapman, biologist, expresses the view of U.S. Fish and Wildlife on Linger Longer's initial town center proposal at the Jekyll Island Authority and Linger Longer Communities public input session, November 14. http://www.savejekyllisland.org/ EnvUSfishandW.html (accessed March 27, 2009).

Cooper Carry. 2006? *Jekyll Island development plan and design guidelines.* Document prepared for the Jekyll Island State Park Authority.

Cordell, H. Ken. 2008. Comments written for Jekyll Island Authority public hearing on the Bleakly Advisory Group financial analysis. Electronic copy sent to author.

————. 2009. Review of Jekyll Island State Park analysis of long-term impacts of development (As submitted by Bleakly Advisory Group, February 2009), February 12. Electronic copy sent to author.

Crompton, John. 2007 In: Constance T. F. de Brun, ed. 2007. *The economic benefits of land conservation*, The Trust for Public Land. San Francisco CA, 1-7.

Driver, B.L. 1999. Management of public outdoor recreation and the related amenity resources for the benefits they provide. In Cordell, H. Ken. 1999. *Outdoor Recreation in American Life*. Champaign, IL: Sagamore Publishing, 2-15.

Duncan, D. 2009. *The national parks: America's best idea*. New York: Alfred A. Knopf.

Egan, David. 2008. Jekyll Island revitalization, but sensitively. *Atlanta Journal Constitution*, February 11.

Egan, Mindy. 2009. Unpublished letter to Mike Hodges and members of the Jekyll Island Authority Conservation Committee, January 12.

Escambia County (Florida) Extension Service. 2009. http://escambia. ifas.ufl.edu/marine/aboutnests.htm (accessed August 3, 2009).

Federal Highway Administration. 1996. *Public involvement techniques for transportation decisionmaking*. http://www.fhwa.dot.gov/reports/ pittd/cover.htm (accessed July 31, 2008).

Ferguson, Anna. 2009a. Contract gives developer options, but board makes decision, *Brunswick News*, January 2.

————. 2009b. Jekyll Island moves on plans, *Brunswick News,* March 11. http://www.thebrunswicknews.com/story/printer/bid-KK (accessed March 11, 2009).

Filippova, Olga. 2009. The influence of submarkets on water view house price premiums. *International Journal of Housing Markets and Analysis* 2, no. 1: 91-105.

Filler, Daniel. n.d. "Theodore Roosevelt: Conservation as the guardian of democracy." http://pantheon.cis.yale.edu/~thomast/essays/filler/ filler.html (accessed November 7, 2009).

Galis, Leon. 2009. The great Jekyll Island giveaway. *Flagpole*, February 17. http://flagpole.com/Weekly/Comment (accessed March 15, 2009).

Georgia Department of Community Affairs. October 19, 2007. *Georgia coastal comprehensive plan, stakeholder involvement program, Draft*, October 19. http://www.georgiaplanning.com/coastal/Stakeholder%20 Involvement%20Plan.pdf (accessed March 27, 2009).

————. 2007. *Georgia coastal comprehensive plan: Assessment draft*, October 19, http://www.dca.state.ga.us/development/Planning QualityGrowth/programs/Assessment061808FINAL%20 DRAFT_001.pdf (accessed March 27, 2009).

Georgia Department of Natural Resources. March 2007. *Partnering for a prosperous future: A 10-year strategic plan for the Georgia Department of Natural Resources*, March. http://www.gadnr.org/PDF/DNR_ Strategic_Plan_March_2007_Final.pdf (accessed April 4, 2009).

————. 2009a. Indian Springs State Park. http://gastateparks.org/info/indspr/ (accessed October 11, 2009).

————. 2008b. *Statewide Comprehensive Outdoor Recreation Plan 2008-2013*. http://www.gastateparks.org/net/content/go.aspx?s=132975.0.1.5 (accessed March 27, 2009).

Glaspell B., A. Watson, K. Kneeshaw and D. Pendergrast. 2003. Selecting indicators and understanding their role in wilderness experience stewardship at Gates of the Arctic National Park and Preserve. *George Wright Forum* 20, no. 3: 59-71.

Hansen, James V. 2002. Foreword. *Land that we love: Americans talk about America's public lands*. Book published for the Olympic Arts Festival, Salt Lake 2002, n.p., http://publiclands.org/homenew.php? newsid=EpVyulAkypXWqLQBuL&SID=%3Chtml.

Hawkins, Carole. December 26, 2008. Authority keeps lid on Jekyll contract. *Georgia Times-Union*, December 26.

————. 2009a. Jekyll businesses pushed out by retail: Most to stay open in trailers, but one will close and another move. November 27. *Georgia Times-Union*.

————. 2009b. Jekyll retailers wait to see where they'll be in future plans: But where stores will go is mystery. *Georgia Times-Union*, July 27.

————. 2009c. Typo in hotel contract could cost Jekyll Island $90,000. *Georgia Times-Union*, June 2.

Hendee, John C. and Chad P. Dawson. 2002. *Wilderness management: Stewardship and protection of resources and values,* 3rd ed. Golden, CO: Fulcrum Publishing.

Holcombe, Jason. April 2, 2009. State park debate should be no laughing matter. Dublin, Georgia *Courier Herald*. April 2. http://news.mywebpal.com/news_tool_v2.cfm?show=localnews&pnpID=909&NewsID=956408&CategoryID=19877&on=1 (accessed April 2, 2009).

How stuff works. http://www.science.howstuffworks.com/barrier-island.htm (accessed April 12, 2009).

Hunter, John. 2008. "Jekyll Island development: A historic perspective." Jekyll Island blog, March 2. http://blog.jekyllisland.com/in-the-news/just-the-facts/jekyll-island-development-a-historic-perspective/ (accessed November 28, 2009).

In Defense of Place. http://www.defenseofplace.org/index.php.

Information Architecture Institute. 2009. http://iainstitute.org/documents/tools/DesignReviewProcess.doc (accessed October 26, 2009).

Initiative to Protect Jekyll Island. 2009a. http://www.savejekyllisland.org/HHCPjuly14.html (accessed August 10, 2009).

————. 2009b. http://www.savejekyllisland.org/leatherback.html (accessed August 17, 2009).

Institute of Community and Area Development. 1983. *Jekyll Island comprehensive land use plan*. University of Georgia.

Jekyll Island State Park Authority. n.d. Jekyll Island Authority (JIA) board retreat summary, June 17 and 18, 2009, Unpublished document.

————. 1982. Jekyll Island Fact Sheet: July 13. Copy received from the Jekyll Island Authority via Georgia Open Records Act Request.

————. 2008. Jekyll Island revitalization program, revitalization partnering agreement. http://www.jeffchapman.us/partner_agreement.pdf (accessed August 3, 2009).

————. 2009. Meeting minutes, March 9. http://www.savejekyllisland.org/JIAbminMr09.html (accessed May 3, 2009).

Johnston, Lori. 2008. Open government heroes: Babs McDonald and Mindy and David Egan, Jekyll Island activists: How many visitors does the island get? *Atlanta Journal-Constitution,* March 16. http://www.ajc.com/search/content/opinion/stories/2008/03/16/jekyll.html (accessed March 15, 2009).

Jones, Walter C. 2009a. Agencies mull how to comply. *Athens Banner-Herald*, July 23. http://www.onlineathens.com/stories/072309/new_468131399.shtml (accessed August 17, 2009)

———. 2009b. The appointed branch of government wields considerable influence, Morris News Service: Bill Shipp's Insider Advantage Georgia, July 27. http://www.insideradvantagegeorgia.com/restricted/2009/July%2009/7-27-09/Jones_Appointed_Branch72719661.php (accessed July 27, 2009).

Knapp, Marilyn S. 2009. 'Friends' group fearful legislators may still privatize Little Ocmulgee. Dublin, Georgia *Courier Herald*, April 1. http://news.mywebpal.com/news_tool_v2.cfm?pnpID=909&NewsID=956089&CategoryID=19667&show=localnews&om=0 (accessed April 2, 2009).

Krueger, Bob. 2009. Krueger: Jekyll chairman says 'we'll press on.' *Savannah Morning News*, December 19.

Land Policy Institute. 2003. Economic valuation of natural resource amenities: A hedonic analysis of Hillsdale and Oakland counties. Report #3, *Series on Economic Impact and Valuation Studies*, Michigan State University, December 3.

Larrabee, Brandon. 2007. Perdue fingerprints are on Jekyll. *Georgia Times-Union*, July 15. http://www.jacksonville.com.

Lewis, David Rich. 2002. A Utahan and historian considers public lands. *Land that we love: Americans talk about America's public lands.* Book published for the Olympic Arts Festival, Salt Lake 2002, n.p., http://publiclands.org/homenew.php?newsid=EpVyulAkypXWqLQBuL&SID=%3Chtml.

Litman, T. 2007. *Planning principles and practices.* Victoria, Canada: Victoria Transport Policy Institute.

Loomis, John. 1993. *Integrated public lands management: Principles and applications to national forests, parks and wildlife refuges, and BLM Lands.* New York: Columbia University Press.

———. 2002. *Integrated public lands management: Principles and applications to national forests, parks, wildlife refuges, and BLM Lands.* 2nd ed. New York: Columbia University Press.

Loomis, John and Richard Walsh. 1997. *Recreation economic decisions: Comparing benefits and costs.* 2nd ed. State College, PA: Venture Publishing.

Major, Christopher and Kenneth Luscht. 2004. The beach study: An empirical analysis of the distribution of coastal property values. Insurance & Real Estate Department, Pennsylvania State University.

Martin, C. Brenden and June Hall McCash. 2003. From millionaires to the masses: Tourism at Jekyll Island, Georgia. In Starnes, Richard D., ed. *Southern journeys: Tourism, history, and culture in the modern south.* Tuscaloosa and London: Univ. of Alabama Press, 154-176.

Maurer, Stephen G. 2002. A very personal introduction. *Land that we love: Americans talk about America's public lands.* Book published for the Olympic Arts Festival, Salt Lake 2002, n.p., http://publiclands. org/homenew.php?newsid=EpVyulAkypXWqLQBuL&SID=%3Ch tml.

McConnell, Kenneth. 1977. Congestion and willingness to pay: A study of beach use. *Land Economics* 53: 187-195.

McDonald, Barbara. 2009. Opinion: Who really speaks for Georgians on Jekyll's future? *Macon Telegraph*, January 31. http://www.macon. com/203/story/605343.html (accessed March 15, 2009).

Miller, J. Tyler Jr. and Scott Spoolman. 2008. *Environmental science.* Cengage Learning.

Morekis, Jim. 2009. "Johnson declares for governor: Kingston rules out run," April 27, ConnectSavannah.com, http://www.connectsavannah. com/news/article/100578/.

National Park Service. 1997. *The Visitor experience and resource protection (VERP) framework: A handbook for planners and managers.* September. U.S. Department of the Interior, National Park Service, Denver Service Center. http://planning.nps.gov/ document/verphandbook.pdf (accessed October 27, 2009).

———. 2009. "Land and water conservation fund." National Park Service. http://www.nps.gov/ncrc/programs/lwcf/history.html (accessed March 27, 2009).

Newell, Steven. 2008. "Jekyll's maritime forest in danger due to Linger Longer's initial town center proposal." http://www.savejekyllisland. org/EnvMaritimeF.html (accessed March 27, 2009).

Pinchot, Gifford. 1910. *The fight for conservation.* The Gutenberg Project, http://www.gutenberg.org/files/11238/11238-8.txt (accessed November 22, 2009).

Robert Charles Lesser & Co., LLC. 2004. *Jekyll Island 2004 Island-wide master plan update.* http://www.sos.ga.gov/archives/pdf/jekyll_ island_master_plan_update.pdf (accessed March 14, 2009).

Savannah Morning News. 2008. Jekyll Island: Shameful secrecy, December 27. http://savannahnow.com/node/643145 (accessed April 5, 2009).

Schoettle, Taylor. 1996. *A guide to a Georgia barrier island: Featuring Jekyll Island with St. Simons and Sapelo Islands.* St. Simons, GA: Watermarks Publishing.

Seiler, Michael J., Michael T. Bond, and Vicky L. Seiler. 2001. The impact of world class Great Lakes water views on residential property values. *Appraisal Journal,* July, 287-295.

Shelton, Stacy. Jekyll Island nearing development limit, student researchers says. *Atlanta Journal Constitution,* December 17.

Sierra Club. 2008. Sierra Club legislative news, April 10. http://www. savejekyllisland.org/Leg.html (accessed April 2, 2009).

Smith, Wilson. October 12, 2007. "Perdue, Mercer Reynolds, Jekyll Island & money: Hanky panky in Georgia politics." October 12. http://www.whatisgoinon.com/ (accessed November 10, 2007).

———. 2008a, April 1. "What is goin on?" http://www.whatisgoinon. com/?s=jekyll+island/ (accessed May 15, 2008).

———. April 14, 2008b. "Jekyll Island: A hopeful reprieve." April 14. http://www.whatisgoinon.com/?s=jekyll+island (accessed March 15, 2009).

———, 2008c. "When it comes to Jekyll Island, the only good Republican is a co-conspirator!" October 4. http://www.whatisgoinon. com/?s=jekyll+island (accessed March 15, 2009).

———. 2009a. "Jewel in the loop." January 8. http://www.whatisgoinon. com/?s=jekyll+island (accessed March 15, 2009).

————. 2009b. "Remember these words: I don't care how much they make!" January 8. http://www.whatisgoinon.com/?s=podcast+jekyll+island (accessed March 15, 2009).

Stamski, Rebecca. 2005. *The impacts of coastal protection structures in California's Monterey Bay National Marine Sanctuary.* Marine Sanctuaries Conservation Series MSD-05-3. U.S. Department of Commerce, National Oceanic and Atmospheric Administration, National Ocean Service, Office of Ocean and Coastal Resource Management, Marine Sanctuaries Division, February. http://sanctuaries.noaa.gov/special/con_coast/stamski.pdf (accessed October 10, 2009).

Starr, Mary. 2006. Jekyll awaiting rebound. *Brunswick News*, May 1.

Stepzinski, Teresa. April 26, 2009. Uncharted: Biologists find rare ecosystem on Jekyll — Individually, the plants are common, but together, "it's kind of rare." *Georgia Times-Union*, April 26. http://www.savejekyllisland.org/PlantCommunity.html. (accessed May 9, 2009).

Taylor, L. and V.K. Smith. 2000. Environmental amenities as a source of market power. *Land Economics* 76, no. 4: 550-568.

Teegardin, Carrie. 2009. Critic says Jekyll Island deal "stinks really, really bad." *Atlanta Journal Constitution*, March 1. http://www.ajc.com/news/content/metro/stories//2009/03/01/jekyll_island_development.html%3Fcxntlid%3Dhomepage_tab_newstab%26imw%3DY (accessed March 14, 2009).

Townsend, Billy. 2001. *History of the Georgia state parks and historic sites division*, October 29. http://www.gastateparks.org/content/georgia/parks/75th_Anniv/parks_history.pdf (accessed March 14, 2009).

USDA Forest Service. 2007. *The greatest good: A Forest Service centennial film.* http://www.fs.fed.us/greatestgood/ (accessed April 12, 2009).

————. 2008. "Questions and answers about the new planning rule." http://www.fs.fed.us/emc/nfma/includes/planning_rule/08_pr_q&as.pdf (accessed November 22, 2009).

Weather.com. 2008. *Where did the beaches go?* Forecast Earth (video), August 2. http://climate.weather.com/video/?clip=11080 (accessed April 4, 2009).

YouTube. "Rediscover Jekyll Island Public Input Sessions." November 20, 2008. http://www.youtube.com/watch?v=mSdrurc7wEY (Part 1), http://www.youtube.com/watch?v=YvERm53ct1Q (Part 2), http://www.youtube.com/watch?v=--gJhlJdg-E (Part3), http://www.youtube.com/watch?v=7BOoztZytS4 (Part 4), http://www.youtube.com/watch?v=c2LTc-668-U (Part 5). Accessed January 13, 2010.

Appendix 1
Signposts for Jekyll's Future

This information and commentary was retrieved from www.savejekyllisland.org, the Web site of the Initiative to Protect Jekyll Island.

The Jekyll Development Picture

As of August 5, 2009, a total of 1,050 new hotel rooms, condominiums and timeshares are planned, approved, or under construction for Jekyll Island. The breakdown is as follows:

Timeshares and condominiums:

- 160 Town center timeshares [construction supposed to begin in 2010]

- 75 Town center condos [construction supposed to begin in 2010]

- 127 Canopy Bluff condos [initial proposal now under revision]

- 80 Oceanfront Resort condos [under construction; completion in Sept. 2009]

- 28 Georgia Coast condos [initial proposal now under revision]

- 80 Jekyll Ocean Oaks condos [plan yet to be released]
- 550 = total number of new timeshare/ condominium units

Hotels:

- 200 rooms — Town center mid-scale hotel [construction to begin in 2010]
- 150 rooms — Town center economy hotel [construction to begin in 2010]
- 300 rooms — Canopy Bluff Resort [replacement for the Buccaneer Resort; initial proposal is currently under revision; update, September 2009]
- 135 rooms — Hampton Inn & Suites [replacement for the Holiday Inn; currently under construction; scheduled to open in January 2010]
- 105 rooms — Inn & Cottages at Georgia Coast [replacement for the Georgia Coast Inn; original proposal is now under revision]
- 180 rooms — Jekyll Oceanfront Resort [construction due to begin in September 2009]
- 1,050 = total number of new hotel rooms

The new condos, time-shares and hotel rooms listed above will bring Jekyll's total number of lodging and residential units to 3,313, which represents a forty-four percent increase over the all-time high figure of 2,303 total units reached back in the 1990s.

Additional development is called for in the Jekyll Island Authority's February 2009 "Business Plan and Visitation Analysis," bringing the total lodging/residence inventory to 4,100 units by the year 2023, a sixty percent increase over the all-time high. Presumably, the additional units will come from:

- The reconstruction/expansion of the Oceanside Inn and Suites

- The construction of condos or villas within the golf course complex

Appendix 2
Environmental Effects Report Checklist

Georgia Environmental Policy Act

Project No. _____

Project Name: _____

For each of the following area types, the checklist asks if the area is affected and if so, how severely (Minor, Median, Major, and Unknown). (Emphasis is mine)

AREA TYPE
Wetlands
Flood Plain/River Corridor
Water Supply
Water Resources
Groundwater Recharge
Storm Water
Air Quality
Solid Wastes
Soil Stability/Erodability
Protected Mountains
Protected Species
Critical Habitats

Historical
Archeological
Parks/Recreation
Energy Supplies
Beaches
Dunes
Shoreline
Coastal Marshland
Forest Land
Barrier Island
Aquatic Life/Trout Streams

Appendix 3
Georgia Open Records Act Request Template

Note: The Jekyll Island Authority has requested a shorter version of this request. They ask that any requests simply be identified as Georgia Open Records Act requests, and they will honor them as such.

Your name and address

OPEN RECORDS ACT REQUEST

Date

Name and address (Jones Hooks, Jekyll Island Authority)

Dear [name]:

This is a public record request for a hard copy of:

[This paragraph should contain a detailed description of exactly which documents are being requested.]

As you know, the Georgia Open Records Act states reasonable charges may be assessed "for search, retrieval, and other direct administrative costs for complying with a request under this Code section. The hourly charge shall not exceed the salary of the lowest paid full-time employee who, in the discretion of the custodian of the records, has the necessary skill and training to perform the request; provided, however, that no charge shall be made for the first quarter hour." O.C.G.A. §§ 50-18-71(d).

I am prepared to pay reasonable search and retrieval fees if necessary. As you know, advance payment is not required under the Act. O.C.G.A. §§ 50-18-71(g). Instead, once documents are requested, charges for all costs incurred by your agency can be collected in the same manner as taxes due. O.C.G.A. §§ 50-18-71(g).

In order to make such a fee request, however, your agency must first notify me of the estimated cost of the copying, search, retrieval and other authorized fees before they are incurred. O.C.G.A. §§ 50-18-71.2.

If my request is denied in whole or in part, the law requires your agency to justify all deletions by reference to exemptions of the Georgia Open Records Act, specifying code section, subsection and paragraph. O.C.G.A. §§ 50-18-72(h). The law also requires you to release all segregable portions of otherwise exempt material. O.C.G.A. §§ 50-18-72(g).

Also, the Open Records Act sets fines up to $100 for any person who fails to provide a requested public document within three (3) business days, unless there are out-of-the-ordinary extenuating circumstances. O.C.G.A. §§ 50-18-74. Therefore, I will expect your agency to produce the requested records within the three-day limit or give written reasons why not, and the specific date the records will be available. O.C.G.A. §§ 50-18-70(f)

Thank you for your assistance. Should your have any questions, please do not hesitate to contact me at [phone number] or via email at [email address].

Best regards,

YOUR NAME, ADDRESS, AND EMAIL

.

Appendix 4
The State Senate Economic Development Committee

On February 28, 2008 the Senate's Economic Development Committee killed legislation introduced by Senator Jeff Chapman (R-Brunswick) that would have prohibited development along the park's remaining open beachfront and promoted Jekyll's affordability for average income citizens. Below is a list of the members of the Senate Economic Development Committee.

Chip Pearson (R-Dawsonville) — Did not vote but opposed the bills
Office phone: 404 656 9221

Who Voted Against Senator Chapman's proposed legislation?

Joseph Carter (R-Tifton)
Office phone: 404 651 7738

George Hooks (D-Americus)
Office phone: 404 656 0065

Bill Jackson (R-Appling)
Office phone: 404 656 5114

Jeff Mullis (R-Chickamauga)
Office phone: 404 656 0057

Jack Murphy (R-Cumming)
Office phone: 404 656 7127

Chip Rogers (R-Woodstock)
Office phone: 404 463 1378

Nancy Schaefer (R-Turnersville)
Office phone: 404 463 1367

Who Voted For Senator Chapman's proposed legislation?

Robert Brown (D-Macon)
Office phone: 404 656 5035

Ed Tarver (D-Augusta)
Office phone: 404 656 0340
(Note: Ed Tarver left the Georgia General Assembly
in late 2009 to become U.S. Attorney for the Southern
District of Georgia.)

Appendix 5
Jekyll Island Authority Board Members (as of October 2009) and Their Professional Affiliations

Robert Krueger: President and CEO, ComSouth Corp; Board of Directors, Georgia Chamber of Commerce; Chairman, Middle Georgia Regional Development Authority

Benjamin Porter: Partner in SGAP Inc., Properties (Real Estate); Board of Directors, Security Bank Holding Company [bank closed in 2009]

Homer "Buddy" DeLoach: Chairman and CFO, Martin Insurance Agency

Michael Hodges: Director, President, and CEO of First Bank of Brunswick; President, Golden Isles Financial Holdings; former Chair, Brunswick-Golden Isles Chamber of Commerce

Chris Clark: Commissioner, Georgia Department of Natural Resources; (former) Deputy Commissioner of Global Commerce, Georgia Department of Economic Development; (former) Executive Director, Georgia Environmental Facilities Authority

Sybil Lynn: Business Owner (restaurant); (former member) Industrial Development Authority

Samuel Kellett: Founder and President of Kangaroo Bob's, an interactive child learning center

Stephen Croy: President, Croy Realty Group; President, Old South Land Company; Managing member, Belfast Investment Group

Richard Royal: President and Owner, Royal Investments, Inc.